Stop Overthinking, Master Your Emotions & Start Taking Action

The Ultimate Guide to Stop Unproductive Thoughts, Beat Negativity and Unlock Your Unlimited Potential by Taking Decisive Action

by

BRILLIANT THINKING

Contents

| Part 1 | Understanding & Solving Overthinking

Section 1: What Is Overthinking

The mind is a wonderful thing—from the ability to imagine, playback a fond memory, memorize a great quote from a book, and understand or interpret otherwise complicated and abstract things; indeed, it is incredible. But the mind, like all things, was not designed to be perfect. It has its faults, including one's tendency to overthink.

In a nutshell, overthinking is defined as the tedious and futile process of thought. The definition alone sounds exhausting as it actually is: the incessant and needless inability of a person to stop himself from worrying about the same thing over and over again, to no avail. However, one may argue that the mind is explicitly built to think. After all, it's the powerhouse of the entire body; the mind sends signals to your nerves to move your limbs, speak up, and even make crucial decisions. But the word "over," being the preceding word of overthinking, is to be taken literally: it simply means too much.

The monotony of the process, or rather, the cycle, is what makes overthinking over-thinking. It's worrying about one thing for an unhealthy period of time, only to come out without a solution and with more anxiety than before; these circumstances are what sets it apart from mere thinking. But, of course, everyone pondered the things they could've done differently. It's human nature to overanalyze and second guess, but what isn't is letting these nagging thoughts affect your life negatively.

To illustrate, imagine yourself walking into the belly of a forest. You pass by a few trees, look back, and still see the road behind you. Then, for no rational reason, you continue moving forward—this time, the trees are taller, and the light is dimmer; the sunlight is hindered by the prominent crowns of green above you. Now, you start to get worried. Still, you continue on the same path simply because you don't know what else to do. The dusk has been swallowed up by the evening; the trees are inseparable from all other shadows of the night. Every crunch of gravel beneath your feet and every twig breaking makes you want to jump out of your skin. For a while, you were in deep. But, by the time you get out, you feel more helpless than relieved. Why? Because you could've turned around the first chance you got before you lost your way, but you didn't do it. You didn't, simply because you couldn't.

This, figuratively, is what overthinking looks and feels like—overthinking is without rhyme or reason. Like the devil on your shoulder, it reminds you of the things that once upset you, angered you, or made you feel uncomfortable. It makes you imagine the worst things that could happen to you right now, tomorrow, or even months from now. It's carrying a glass half-full in one hand; the first minute, light. The next hour? Painful but tolerable. But the next day, paralyzing. You may think your brain can handle it right now, but like a numbing hand, it will soon give out.

But from all the definitions of overthinking, the important one is this: overthinking is a habit. The good thing is habits can be unlearned. So, unlearn reliving these destructive thoughts and ease your mind before it gives out.

Section 2: Signs You Are An Overthinker

Have you ever suddenly recalled a disagreement from a few months ago? How about being unable to sleep in the wee hours of the night or waking up in the midst of it so that you can freak yourself out over tomorrow's presentation? How anxious were you during these times? Does the adjective 'worried' sound like an understatement? While at it, did you come up with a resolution to these anxieties and worries? If you just answered no, you might be an overthinker.

But fear not, for being an overthinker is not something to be ashamed of. In fact, research spearheaded by the University of Michigan revealed that 73% of people aged 25 to 35 are overthinkers, and 52% of people aged 45 to 55 also are. Hence, if you think about it, overthinking seems like an unprecedented epidemic. However, it's almost nothing special—that is, until it begins to impair your way your life.

So, are you an overthinker? These are ten telling signs that you are:

1. *You replay embarrassing moments in your head.*

    When people say, "there's no point crying over spilled milk," they mean nothing good comes out of fretting over an unfortunate event that has already taken place. But to you, this idiomatic expression holds no power over your emotions. Instead, you relive the moment you spilled the milk, hoping in vain to go back in time before it was spilled. Although you know thinking about it is pointless, you continue to replay it in your mind countlessly and tirelessly, not just the memory itself but also the feelings of guilt, shame, and regret. All over again. And again. And again.

2. *You have a hard time falling asleep because your brain is too awake.*

    Despite the efforts to turn off the lights, meditate or pray, and even count sheep, you just can't bring yourself to fall asleep effortlessly. Unfortunately, your brain keeps you away from your needed sweet slumber. Instead of falling asleep right off the bat, your brain has its long list of agendas to discuss during these unholy hours—nagging, demanding, and difficult to ignore.

3. *You ask yourself "what if" a little too much for your own good.*

   What if I moved to another city? What if I took that master's degree? What if I saved more money? What if I didn't date this person? What if I exercised, ate well, and drank more water? What if I stopped asking all these what-if questions? You can't.

4. *You read between the lines in search of hidden meanings—even when there aren't.*

   So, your friend sent you a message without an emoji in it? She's probably sick of you. Your boss increased his tone to you by an octave higher? You're probably getting fired. Your lover didn't call you first thing in the morning? He's probably cheating on you. These are some thoughts that plague your mind. What should be irrelevant details in your social interactions seem a concern to you.

5. *You replay a conversation and wish you had said things better.*

   After an argument, you find yourself sitting with yourself, recalling the bitter, anger-fueled conversation you just had—or had a week ago—and suddenly, you think of all the better comebacks you could've said but didn't. Gosh, how you wish you could go back in time just to win that argument, if not for your sloppy replies the first time around.

6. *You are unable to live down your mistakes.*

   Everyone makes mistakes; it's human nature. But your human nature also never lets you forget every single mistake you've ever made in your entire life. Remember when you squeaked during recitations in fifth grade? Of course, you still do.

7. *You have a habit of recalling things that bothered or offended you.*

   So, your coworker made a sarcastic remark about your presentation? The cashier from the grocery rolled her eyes while you checked out? Your Uber driver didn't greet you when you got on the ride? How long have you been thinking and pondering about these things?

8. *You space out at any time of the day so you can worry about things that have happened and things that might happen.*

   Earth to you, they always say. Your head is always up in the stratosphere without consciously knowing that you have spaced out. While you do so, you remember something from the past that makes you uncomfortable, or you think of something in the future that makes you worried. When it happens, it happens without warning and sends your mood in the wrong direction.

9. *You worry about things you can't control.*

   You can't control the things that happen around you, but you can control how you react to them. For example, if the weather forecast says there's a chance of rain, bring an umbrella. If the news informs you of a traffic jam on your usual route, take a detour. If your go-to café closed down, get your coffee elsewhere. Easier said than done, right? Because to you, the weather, the traffic, and the economy are also your concern.

10. *You can't get your mind off all your worries, no matter how hard you try.*

    You're finally at your wits' end with the endless worrying, slowly crippling you from the fully-functioning person you were, but even at your wits' end, your mind takes control. In a battle between you and your brain, the latter always wins. So, here you are again down the rabbit hole of overthinking.

If these signs apply to you, I suggest you don't overthink it, but it's probably too late. Instead, we must delve into these personal struggles and see them as opportunities to learn and grow. We must never forget that the first step to managing the problem is acknowledging that there is one.

Section 3: What Causes Overthinking

At one point in your life, you probably told yourself that you must stop overthinking. Maybe you have acknowledged how unproductive and time-consuming it is to worry and ruminate on something you have no power over—like the past and the future. In recognizing this, the next step is asking, why are you overthinking in the first place? But it's a question that's too difficult to conclude, especially when it happens automatically and habitually, like a self-defense mechanism. So instead of making a solution, you sit on your problems, hoping they will disappear.

But the causes of overthinking are no mystery; it isn't as mystical as the unsolved questions on consciousness itself. Overthinking is highly related to poor decision-making, anxiety, depression, and lack of sleep. In this Chapter, we discuss the psychological causes of overthinking.

1. *Early Development*
   Habits develop over time, and since overthinking is a habit, most people struggling with it develop it during the early stages of their lives or childhood. This mostly

happens when a child is exposed to challenging situations growing up—where they are forced to think excessively over these experiences as they happen and after.

Since children are innately unable to manage their emotions appropriately, the thoughts that come with the negative experiences are hardly resolved by themselves; hence, they start to overthink and fail to solve the issue actively.

The theory of nature versus nurture indeed plays a role in a person's overall development. In most cases, the traits they developed seep into their adult lives and continue to affect them.

2. *Control and Certainty*

    In the stages of grief, the first stage is known to be "denial," or the refusal of one person to accept or admit the occurrence of something, perhaps death or separation. But grieving or not, denial has become a self-defense mechanism for several people. Instead of confronting reality, they refuse to believe in it simply because believing is the first step to accepting...accepting that you no longer have control over the situation.

    If there is anything that people hate, it's feeling helpless and uncertain. So, to momentarily cope with the inability to do and know anything for sure, people think and worry about the situation. They play this situation in their heads repeatedly, pretending they can still do something about it, that the problem can still be solved if they just think it through. But deceiving yourself that you still have control is not the cure to the problem. The real cure is cozying up to the reality that things happen when they happen before you even get to know them. Life is meant to be unpredictable.

3. *Behavior and Personality*

    Each person sees the world from a different perspective. In comparison, some people don't think twice about leaving the kitchen faucet on, and some check on it twice. While some see the picture as it is, some have complicated interpretations. Some people are obsessive perfectionists, some overgeneralize everything, and some are afraid of conflict and rejection—the circle of life, only rougher.

    By this, we mean that overthinking is accompanied by a person's already-developed behavior and personality. Most perfectionists have a difficult time moving forward from things because they feel as if something isn't as perfect as they hoped it would be. They worry about minor details because everything has to be up to their standards— even the things they have no control over. These people are also incapable of tolerating anything less than "perfect," so they go around trying to improve everything in their heads.

    The same goes for people who overgeneralize or think bad luck in one aspect of life means bad luck in everything else. Poisonous thought is the best fuel for overthinking. Instead of brushing off one failure as just one failure, it affects everything else. You start to think failing a subject means never graduating, not getting a good job, and living in poverty. To someone who overgeneralizes and overthinks, everything is a problem.

    Lastly, people who fear conflict and rejection find themselves avoiding conflict and rejection. How? By overthinking all the ways they can avoid them, even if it means they

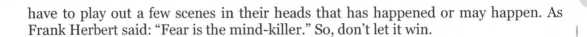

have to play out a few scenes in their heads that has happened or may happen. As Frank Herbert said: "Fear is the mind-killer." So, don't let it win.

4. *False Sense of Gain*

Realistically speaking, people only do things they benefit from—and it isn't self-serving to say it out loud because everybody else does it. The same thing goes for overthinking. People overthink because they gain something from it. Or at least they believe they do.

When a person overthinks, he can convince himself to postpone doing something that he dreads doing in the first place. It's like a mental pep talk, but instead of pumping you up, it gives you an excellent excuse to procrastinate. It could also make you seem more "vulnerable," thereby gaining attention and sympathy from the people around you. And who doesn't like being the centerpiece in the room?

What overthinking really gives you is a false sense of gain. You may think you're getting something out of it, but in reality, you're like a dog catching its tail—going around in circles without resolve.

Although these are just some recognized causes of overthinking, the list continues to pile on. The bottom line is that the ability to identify the cause of your overthinking is likewise the ability to unlearn it slowly.

Section 4: Overthinking Affects Your Personality

As discussed earlier, personality and overthinking seem entangled in more ways than one. So it would appear that overthinking shapes one's personality and vice versa. For example, it can make a rather lively person detached. Happy to depressed. Optimistic to hesitant. Confident to self-doubting. But how does overthinking change a person's personality? Simply put, overthinking starts a hostile takeover inside your mind—like a virus compromising your immune system.

During said "hostile takeover," your mind lets down its guards to make way for your thoughts. Too much of your thoughts. It presents several situations in your head, then a greater number of decisions to choose from. Then, it clouds your judgment and makes you lose focus on that one good choice, making you indecisive. In effect, your brain exerts more effort than usual. The more effort it exerts, the less creative it gets. Studies show that creativity springs from the calmness of the mind, and this is something that overthinking robs you off.

But it's not just your decision-making and creativity that overthinking impairs. Evidently, it ultimately affects your life. The bridge between physical and mental wellness is closer than we imagine. The phenomena of psychosomatic disorder now exist, whereby your mind produces physical symptoms such as breathing problems, migraines, and even ulcers. The most straightforward explanation for this is the most obvious: a person must be mentally well to be physically well. However, some of the manifestations of overthinking are not necessarily health-related but more behavioral.

A person who overthinks becomes quickly exhausted since his mental energy is drained from all the pointless thinking. He also starts to withdraw from his social circle because it is easier to avoid people than deal with them on top of the endless, nagging thoughts in his head. As a result, he becomes aloof and easily irritated. These are only a few of the many effects overthinking has on a person's personality.

Like the flu, overthinking gets worse when left unmanaged and untreated. Although thinking forms a vital part of living, it is crucial to realize when thinking has become overthinking. What started as a harmless habit can alter your personality and affect your social interaction.

Section 5: Effects Of Overthinking

Now that you have an in-depth comprehension of what overthinking is, it's time to discuss the more negative aspect of overthinking. The truth is, the harm overthinking brings about outweighs its benefits, if there are even any. This time, we ask the question, how bad can overthinking get? How will it affect my life short-term and long term? Can overthinking kill me? Probably! As Mark Twain stated, "too much of anything is bad."

So, let's begin uncovering the dangers of overthinking.

1. *Poor quality sleep*

    We know that overthinking tends to occur just when we decide to sleep. Perhaps, the mind misinterprets the calmness of the night as the opportunity to hear itself think. This is when we recall embarrassing moments, worry about insignificant details like locking the front door, or get nervous about future affairs in our lives, like tomorrow's business pitch. Doing this makes a person uneasy to the point that it spoils the body's resting state.

    As an effect, during our waking hours, insufficient sleep manifests as a lack of energy, moodiness, slowed thinking and reaction time, inattentiveness, bad decision-making, and even worsened memory. In addition, sleep deprivation also contributes to a list of health problems like cardiovascular diseases, diabetes, obesity, immunodeficiency, and more.

2. *Inconsistent appetite*

    Since overthinking drastically affects a person's mood, one may lose or suddenly have an increased appetite. While anxious, eating becomes less of a priority—for some. To others, eating becomes a coping mechanism to distract oneself from the demanding and overwhelming thoughts inside your head. But eating less or eating more without a proper schedule or a healthy meal plan does more harm than good, especially in physical fitness.

3. *Chemical imbalance*

Chemical imbalance has been scientifically proven to damage a person's brain structure in terms of processing memories and regulating feelings and emotions. One of the causes of chemical imbalance is building up negative thoughts in the brain, which clouds its ability to differentiate hypothetical stress from actual stress. As a result, instead of the brain focusing on real stress, it overlaps the problem-solving function of the brain with made-up stress borne out of overthinking. This was according to Rick Hansen, a neuropsychologist from UC Berkeley.

4. *Mental illnesses*

Overthinking is a well-known risk factor and symptom for the onset of mental disorders, including major depressive disorder, anxiety, and personality disorders. The Journal of Abnormal Psychology presented that overthinking increases the risk of suffering from mental health problems such as depression, anxiety, bipolar disorder, post-traumatic stress disorder, and even borderline personality disorder.

The association of stressful life events, overthinking, and mental health disorders have long been correlated.

5. *Shorter lifespan*

Research now reveals that neural activity emerges as a new character in human aging and longevity. This means a person's brain activity can either shorten or extend his or her lifespan. Studies suggest that persons who suppress overactivity of the brain extend their life, while excessive brain activity can cause shorter life spans. In a sense, long-term overthinking expedite the aging of the human brain, making it more vulnerable to disorders like dementia and epilepsy. Although it is not definite that overthinking can kill you faster than average, your brain activity plays a significant role in your lifespan.

Harvard School found that people who died younger, compared to the other study participants, had lower levels of protein in their brains. This certain protein aids with the brain's resting state—its depletion is directly related to excessive brain activity like habitual overthinking.

At the moment, you may consider overthinking as a mere nuisance and impediment to your daily life. Still, the persistence of it for long periods actually impacts your physical health, mental health, and, ultimately, your life.

Section 6: Effective Ways To Stop and Overcome Overthinking

Life as we know it is already difficult as it is. Fused with embarrassing moments, bad experiences, things beyond our control, and future uncertainties, our minds often find themselves in a loop of endless thinking—unhealthy thinking. If you think about it, it's pretty ironic that when we only have ourselves, we are also *against* ourselves. But nobody has lived long enough to say: "life is a walk in the park," because it isn't. Unless this walk is a seven-day hike without water and this park is a 'Jurassic' park. Sadly, sometimes the enemy is also us. And now, overthinking has taken a toll on our lives physically, mentally, and socially. So, it's time to consider some ways to stop overthinking—or at least control and manage its occurrence. So, we've rounded up some tips to prevent or overcome overthinking.

1. *Create healthy distractions*

    By nature, overthinking is also a distraction from your day-to-day life; it keeps you occupied for fruitless reasons and is an unhealthy distraction that uses up much of your time and energy. Thus, knowing when the overthinking start is crucial, so you can actively combat these thoughts with other distractions, only this time, healthier.

    Instead of wallowing in the dark corners of your mind, be present or practice mindfulness—being mindful of right now and what's happening at the moment. If you are in a social function, interact. If you are at home, converse with a family member. Being present means enjoying things as they happen, watching them unfold by the minute. But being present also means being able to take care of things that need your urgent attention, like your state of mind. When overthinking becomes unbearable, be present for yourself—find someone to confide in or someone who can help you distract yourself from the urge to go down the rabbit hole of overthinking. Investing your time with the people around you and living in the moment are better ways to spend your time. The art of mindfulness allows you to separate yourself from the past to the present, so you can give attention to what you're faced with right now.

    Furthermore, it would help if you also enjoyed the things that you do. You should move around, unplug from your devices, and bathe in the graciousness of nature. Maybe read a book, exercise, meditate, and go for a walk—do something else apart from overthinking. More so, incorporate these positive "acts of calmness" in your routine to give overthinking lesser wiggle room. It's a fact of science that overthinking occurs less when the mind rests.

2. *Redirect your focus*

    Life has ways of bringing you down—brutal and cruel, to say the least. It can get so depressing sometimes that you find yourself asking hard questions that you only have worse answers to…if you can even answer them. And now, life has brought you to your knees, only so you take a moment to get a grip back up. This is why changing or redirecting your focus is the newest must-have skill. Redirecting your focus is a small act of changing your mindset, but it's more than mental activity. Instead of avoiding the hard questions, you must learn to ask them better. Ask better questions to get better answers.

    Focusing on something else isn't always the key. Distraction works, but not all of the time. Sometimes, it only shifts your focus on the wrong things. Some anxieties are more than just unnecessary voices in our heads; sometimes, it asks valid questions. But how can we deal with it if the voice forces a bitter pill down our throats? The secret?

Rephrase the question better. Instead of "why are you so irresponsible?" Ask yourself, "how can I be more responsible?" Ask better, literally.

You see, the brain is made for solving problems, but you need to ask it better. How you talk to your inner self can improve how you live your life. Some pointers to redirect your focus is asking yourself properly instead of demanding. Ask yourself "how," not "why." Focus on what you want to do and what you want to accomplish more than focusing on the struggles that come with it. Immerse yourself in the beauty of possibilities—the beauty of the future. Talk to yourself kindly; use questions that trigger positive emotions.

These are some more examples of asking better:

"Why is the weather so gloomy?" to "How can I still make the most out of this day?"

"Why am I so lazy?" to "How can I start doing more?"

"Why is my room such a mess?" to "How can I clean it up?"

"Why does my body feel weak?" to "How about I begin exercising?"

"Why am I always overloaded with work?" to "How can I manage my time better?"

"Why am I always tired?" to "How can I distribute my energy better?"

"Why do I feel so lonely?" to "How about I take the time to see my family and friends?"

"Why do I often feel discouraged?" to "How can I reconnect with my spirituality again?"

"Why am I jealous and insecure?" to "How can I feel more confident with myself?"

"Why am I unhappy with my life?" to "How can I start appreciating my life more?"

Redirecting your focus into a kinder way of speaking to yourself can do so much for your mind. What makes overthinking unpleasant is how much work it feels like, like a nagging boss who never saw how hard you work. So, what happens if that "boss" speaks to you kindly? The work feels much better to do. So, change your focus like that.

3. *Be kinder to yourself.*

What overthinking actually does to you is ruin your self-image and your self-confidence. By introducing you to negative thoughts that make you question yourself—your capabilities and your decisions, you slowly start to hate yourself. Self-doubt and guilt are often aftereffects of overthinking. This is why it's essential to love, be kind to, and forgive yourself. It may sound cliché, but a little bit of self-love goes a long way.

How? First, by focusing on what you can control. When your mind starts to crush you with the weight of your fears and anxieties, identify what triggers these thoughts and ask yourself, "what do I have control over?" By redirecting your thoughts to your power, you remind yourself that you are capable, unlike what overthinking wants you to believe.

Some of the things you can control are your "what if" questions and the story you tell yourself. For example, instead of asking, "what if I resigned last year?" change it to: "what if I seek better opportunities this year?" Another is the story you tell yourself. Instead of saying, "I hit rock bottom because I'm unskilled and incapable," tell yourself, "Hitting rock bottom means there's only one way out, and it's up." Empower yourself with optimistic thoughts that encourage you to act. After all, if your mind makes you question yourself, you can counter it by convincing your mind otherwise. Remember, you are capable and worth more than your mind tells you; this is your daily mantra. But if fighting your thoughts sounds difficult to you, then don't. It may seem counterintuitive, but accepting and interpreting these thoughts differently has a paradoxical effect. Instead of getting frustrated that you can't stop thinking about this one thing, appreciate it; find it interesting. In a way, you become kinder to your own mind by thinking it's not the antagonist. The "mental villain" loses its power over your emotions by committing yourself to kinder thoughts. It's the same with people who have done us wrong. It's better to accept they did what they did and move on than plot revenge or make it even. Commitment therapy is not just exposing yourself to the trigger, but embracing it for your well-being.

Being kinder to yourself is easier than it sounds. Some of these acts, such as imperfections and intuition, are already handed to us by nature itself. The thing is, the only person begging you to be perfect is you. Once you realize that there is no such thing as the one perfect answer in life, you learn to work through it. Flaws can be improved and patched through. Perfectionism is not an endearing trait of the successful but a huge roadblock that stops a person from being efficient in making decisions; it's a symptom of overthinking that keeps you from getting things done. If overthinking prevents you from making wise decisions, it also helps to pair your analytical thinking with your gut. "Trust your gut," they said. Because you should. Your intuition is faster and more reliable than rational thoughts alone. Intuition is both ingrained instinct and spontaneous knowledge. So, when your mind is overwhelming you, especially in decision-making, trust your intuition. Don't let your mind make you run around in circles for fear of making the wrong choice. Remember that the correct answer is usually your first answer—the one that your gut already told you.

4. *Study the art of letting go*

Since overthinkers often punish themselves by recalling the past, they exert too much energy on thinking about how they could've done better. But, by doing this, they take no part in setting the past from the present. As a result, the line between yesterday and today gets blurred. The truth is, people find it hard to move past difficult times, such as terminations, breakups, and the death of a family member—and it's all valid. But some people just can't seem to move on from hardships even after a significant amount of time has passed.

It's important to understand that the past can no longer be changed—it's already a part of your history. But the only reason you're still thinking about it with bitterness is that you have yet to realize the real lesson from this experience. Thus, you must look at this experience with fresh eyes and free your mind by accepting it has already happened and positively reinforcing the lesson. Hence, if you broke your mom's favorite vase years ago, the lesson is not that you're clumsy; the lesson is you have to be careful. By relearning your mistakes positively, you let go of your grudge against the past. It's usually the pain from the memory that makes you indifferent toward it. If that pain no longer has power over your emotions, you unburden yourself from taking up a vast mental space that causes you to overthink.

We must realize that when we fail to accept and forgive things that have already happened to us, we are the only ones hurting ourselves. It's a bitter pill to swallow, but the person who fired you and dumped you is probably not thinking about you anymore. They're unbothered by your absence, so you should be too. Even the person who has left this earth doesn't want you putting your life on hold because of their passing; they're probably looking down on you, wishing you'd get back to your usual bright self. When we accept, we reduce matters that our minds can rethink and regret.

5. *Practice gratitude*

While our minds magnify our guilts and regrets, we feel as if our values as persons depreciate—as if we're no longer worthy of a new project, a new relationship, or a new hobby. Just because we didn't do so well the last time we had something like that. Although "think positive" may sound like shallow advice, positivity is more than just a mindset. It's a lifestyle that improves your quality of life. One positive act is being grateful.

For a person who overthinks everything, we're more sorry than grateful half of the time. Sorry that you didn't get the promotion, sorry that you didn't have a better conversation with an old friend, sorry that you didn't win that academic award in school, and sorry that you weren't a better partner, sibling, or daughter. A lot of feeling sorry for yourself contributes heavily to the diminution of your self-worth. So, practice gratitude more. Replace apologies with appreciation.

Being grateful has a wide range of psychological and physical benefits, from becoming more confident to having a healthier outlook in life and even a lighter feeling daily—no more worn-out body due to a worn-out mind. When we practice gratefulness, we rewire our minds to look back at moments without bitterness. When difficult things happen, we become thankful we overcame it rather than sorry it didn't go as planned. Gratefulness can completely change our perspective. So, find something you're grateful for, not things to worry about. It can be the gift of life, your family and friends, your courage, your intellect, or even your mistakes and the lessons that came with them.

6. *Help yourself*

When it comes to the mind, the real secret to recovery is within yourself. Thus, you can only truly tame overthinking by having the will to do so. More than stopping yourself from overthinking, you must be proactive; practice acts that prevent you from overthinking in the first place.

First, set the alarm for your worry period. Meaning, choose a time in your day as your worry period and start worrying for a maximum of 30 minutes a day only. During this time, start writing down problems. But instead of your usual cycle of realizing these problems, sitting down, and letting them run amok in your head, this time, also write down possible solutions. If the problem is about something you can't control, write down how you'll react when it happens. Being strict with this schedule helps you manage and limit your overthinking. Alongside this, you also have to learn how to prioritize your problems, for some of them are not worth the energy to mull over. Understand that some problems require immediate attention, and some are not problems at all but fragments of the past you haven't settled with.

Apart from setting the alarm for your worry period, determine a time or date for confronting other things, like when to get back to a client or how long it would take you to make an important decision. By putting these things on your calendar, you consciously inspire yourself to make decisions and take action. Deadlines aren't so bad when it helps you stay on track, especially when it's for your mental wellness. Knowing that overthinking can sometimes jeopardize your schedule, reminding yourself of what needs to be done and when to get them done gives you a sense of accountability and responsibility.

7. *Practice empowering postures*

Amy Cuddy presented research that indicated posture could make a person feel more powerful. Although it sounds like pseudoscience, if not placebo, research shows that stance and posture can impact thoughts and behavior. So, fact or fiction? We say fact. In power posing, assuming an open or expansive stance, or making yourself appear bigger and taller, can actually and scientifically make you feel more powerful compared to contracted or reserved poses.

A study was conducted where applicants who assumed power poses did better in interviews than those who didn't. Even students felt more confident when dealing with teachers. The somewhat new trick seems revolutionary in that it can aid in alleviating the symptoms of overthinking; after all, confidence can counter a mind full of self-doubt. And to think it's so simple: just assert a more assertive posture. But if scholars are already acknowledging the connection between posture and emotions, undoubtedly, the dread that comes with overthinking can be reduced by a straight back, a broad chest, and a chin held high.

A perfect illustration would be a game of poker. We all know that bluffing in poker is one way to win or psych the other players into thinking you have better cards. When bluffing, you keep a neutral, relaxed face. You don't bow down your head. You don't slouch. You even lean back and cross your legs, exuding confidence. And when you act confident, you feel confident. So, what if we incorporate these power poses in times of doubt? Or fear? Of cluelessness? Of overthinking? Then, we can trick our minds into thinking we have control over it instead. One esteemed academe said on power poses: "the effect isn't huge, but it's clearly there."

8. *Go to therapy*

What's even more critical in helping yourself is knowing when it's time to seek professional help. For some people, their overthinking has become so rampant that it seems impossible to control it on their own. This is when we should allow ourselves to get help from psychiatrists and therapists.

Talk therapy or Cognitive Behavioral Therapy (CBT) is one of the most common forms of psychotherapy. It aims to manage mental and emotional problems, such as depression and anxiety, grief and stress, and even overthinking. CBT helps a person rewire the negative thoughts in their heads through positive reinforcement or through introducing healthy coping mechanisms that effectively ease worries and anxieties. In addition, it helps identify unhelpful behavioral patterns and allows your therapist to learn these psychological issues better to design the right coping mechanism that will alleviate your symptoms and improve your mental and emotional health.

Simply put, it's the process of identifying your unhealthy habits and reinforcing a better thought process for you. But CBT is not a cure-for-all. It takes several sessions before the most practical advice can be given to you. But definitely, it teaches you better ways to respond to stress and difficult situations apart from overthinking.

But, of course, unlearning the unhealthy habit of overthinking requires patience and dedication. These tips are not meant to change your life and your perspective overnight. But, to properly win against the threats of the mind, we must put in the effort.

Section 7: Visualization To Help Stop Overthinking

In a world where stillness is more of a luxury than necessity, we often find ourselves seeking solace in the most unlikely places—in the company of a beer bottle or beside a stranger on public transport. It's a place where cars never stop running, and people never take a break for themselves. It's a moment when days and nights are neither shorter nor longer; they just overlap with each other. It's a world that seems never to allow its inhabitants to rest their minds.

We often confuse innovation with better quality of life. Sure, now all the information in the world is one touch of a fingertip away. We no longer grind our own coffees or gather firewood to keep warm. But innovation also brought us noise—one that doesn't let you hear your thoughts and one that lets you hear your thoughts too much.

Ignorance is bliss, and when taken figuratively, the life of men before us seem more peaceful. Because today, our minds are loaded with information, emotions, and thoughts that are unnecessary and exhausting. With almost everything at our disposal, our minds are bound to explode. As a result, people today are more worn out mentally and emotionally, and overthinking is one of the most common culprits. On the other hand, now, there are more ways than one to battle overthinking. One of the means to help alleviate the symptoms of overthinking is through a solemn visualization. Basically, it's an exercise that distracts you from your worries and anxieties. Still, more than that, it provides you with the brief opportunity to escape into the ethers of nothingness where your mind can rest.

To begin, find a quiet place to do this exercise. Make sure it's a place where you can relax both your body and mind. Silence is the main requirement for this *guided visualization*.

Once you've come to rest, close your eyes and focus only on this exercise. Listen to your breathing; feel your lungs constrict and expand as you inhale and exhale. Finally, clear your mind from intrusive thoughts and tell them they are not welcome here.

Now that you have eased into the calmness. Release yourself from the tensions of your mind and become a mere observer of your feelings and thoughts; watch your body as you slip further. Appreciate how peaceful it is in your mind right now and how relaxed you are. Indulge in the serenity. Next, meditate on self-forgiveness; tell yourself that it's normal to have these worrying thoughts and that you forgive yourself for having them. Then echo encouraging words to affirm yourself, "I am at peace," "I deserve to be in this relaxed state." Now, imagine a light surrounding you as your mind floats away from the bustle of the earth—the light releases you from your overwhelming thoughts. What color is your light, and how bright is it? Remember this until you return to yourself. As you return, feel oxygen travel from your head to the tip of your toes. Slowly come back to reality—only this time, with a distance between you and your overthinking. Try to keep it that way for the entire day.

So, what is the purpose of this guided visualization? A ten-minute exercise you can incorporate daily? The answer is quite apparent: to ease yourself from the mental fatigue overthinking has brought you.

But if a quiet place is not something accessible to you at the moment, temporary relief from your overthinking can also be done. This time, all you need are your five senses—sight, touch, hearing, smell, and taste. This is what you call *grounding techniques*.

Grounding techniques are exercises that help a person stay "grounded" in the present moment. Research in 2014 concluded that stress reduction strategies such as grounding techniques successfully reduce anxiety, depression, and pain symptoms. Since it's been proven effective in several mental health conditions, the same can be applied to overthinking.

To step back from your negative thoughts, practice the 5-4-3-2-1 technique. Once overthinking kicks in, detach yourself from such thoughts, look around, and focus on the following: 5 things you see, 4 things you feel, 3 things you hear, 2 things you smell, and 1 thing you taste. Doing this allows your focus to shift elsewhere apart from the overwhelming thoughts in your head.

For sense of sight, you could focus on a small object near you, perhaps a particular shaped object in the room, and even your surroundings, like the sky, the clouds, or even trees as they sway along with the wind.

For touch, you can feel the fabric on the clothes you're wearing, touch your hair, or take turns feeling the furniture in the area. You can also put your hands under running water or intertwine your fingers.

For hearing, focus on the sounds and noises surrounding you; the ticking of the clock, the moving cars outside, conversations from the other room, music, singing, and even dogs barking. If you can, listen to yourself breathing.

For smell, take a deep breath and identify the scents around you. Then, if nothing in particular registers in your mind, you can step out of the room to smell freshly-cut grass. You can light a scented candle in your room or open some scented oils. You can even walk into the bathroom to smell some lotion, shampoo, or a soap bar.

Lastly, for the sense of taste, take any food that you can taste easily. For example, put a small amount of sugar or salt on your tongue, or take a piece of gum or mint. If none of these are accessible to you at that particular moment, then recall the distinct flavors of something you've already tasted.

This technique was built to keep you grounded before you lose yourself in the depths of overthinking and strong emotions. Your senses help you return to the present, so try your best to stay there. Fight your mind and refuse to let it wander into the pains of the past and the uncertainty of the future.

Another least popular visualization technique is *asking your subconscious mind*. Since our conscious mind is heavily decorated—or plagued—with thoughts and feelings we already know and fears and expectations we've yet to uncover, simple questions are not answered outright. They can only be done by recalling data from our knowledge and experiences. In other words, the conscious mind has a limited, slower information-processing ability. So, what sets it apart from the subconscious mind? Simple. The subconscious mind is more straightforward, liberal, and sensible—it does not communicate with your experiences and fears when answering questions; it just answers.

Asking the subconscious mind is a unique activity in therapy that requires you to communicate with yourself intimately, mentally speaking. The usual "ask yourself a question" is simplified by asking your subconscious mind the question instead. This means you ask yourself a question, willfully and intently, but directed to the subconscious mind. Ask the question clearly and receive the answer as it is—without interpreting it.

Since the subconscious mind does not dwell on things you already know and feel, the answer comes to you more efficiently. It's one coming from beyond your gut. So when asking your subconscious mind a question, it's necessary to remind yourself that most of the questions you'll ask are things you already know the answer to. Except the subconscious mind gives it to you bluntly, assertively.

This technique requires a bit of practice for you to differentiate the answer between your conscious and subconscious minds. Pro tip: the first answer is usually the one from your subconscious. Another tip: don't taint the literal meaning by reading between the lines or comparing it to a "better" answer. So, when faced with a difficult question about life, sit down, relax, and communicate with your subconscious. Whatever the answer is, accept it. If you can, act on it.

Now that you've been introduced beyond the surface of the mind, the wonders of your imagination, senses, and subconscious allow you more reprieve from the demands and clamor of our perpetually busy lives and exhausted minds.

Section 8: What is Mental Clutter

I'm sure that you found yourself on the brink of a mental breakdown at one point in your life. You probably felt the urge to throw things, scream at the top of your lungs, or walk out in the middle of the day. Maybe you felt this before leaving for the airport, where you still had to pack your best clothes, find your misplaced passport, and contact a trusted dog-sitter. Maybe an hour before a board meeting, you had to fix the venue, prepare the materials, brew the coffee, and make last-minute phone calls to the attendees. Then, on top of whatever you're doing, you're inclined to reply to an important email, call your mom back, and plan your schedule for tomorrow. In the end, your mind is a mess—and this is an understatement.

To you, it feels like a hundred things at once are floating in your head, begging to be given attention. It's an audience of twenty angry men inside your mind who want to speak to the manager—you. It sounds overwhelming, right? Even anxiety-inducing. This, as an illustration, is what mental clutter looks like.

It isn't always negative thoughts that are cluttered in your head, though. Instead, it could be a combination of the positives, the neutrals, the random, and the unnecessary. But when you put all of these ingredients in one pot, the tendency is that it will overflow upon boiling temperature. And this is when you most need to pay attention to your mental wellness.

As human as we are, we all procrastinate. From time to time, we set aside certain things to do, thinking that it isn't a priority if it's a week before the deadline. We push almost everything to the last minute because there are better things to do right now. And we do this for nearly everything. Little do we know, these "small" acts of pushing things further down your schedule are causing traffic among everything else that you've set aside. This could be as insignificant as cleaning out your office desk or as important as getting your annual physical check-up, but as you push them all to one room in your head, you fail to notice how crowded it is in there—

at least until the room explodes. Now, while you're working on today's agenda, your mind suddenly reminds you of the calling card you misplaced on your desk. It suddenly concerns you about the week-old rash on your arm. As a result, now, you can't focus on one thing.

Sadly, decluttering your desk or fixing your schedule is relatively easier than decluttering your mind. Why? Because the mind is more complicated than we think it is. We may believe we've gained control over our brain activity, but it often feels like our minds have their own "mind" controlling us instead and dictating how we should feel. It sends us into a cycle of negativity, restlessness, emptiness, and uncertainty, all in a matter of seconds. The real struggle is not the number of thoughts per se; it's how we entangle ourselves from them—how we differentiate which are worth the energy dealing with and which are merely intrusive distractions.

Mental clutter is the constant battle between you and your mind, or at least the part of your mind that drags you through the thick mud of anxiety, guilt, self-doubt, and many more. It deprives you of mental peace and clarity, as it is simultaneously demanding and chaotic.

Section 9: What Causes Mental Clutter

To further understand the mind, we explore our biology by briefly discussing the physical makeup of the brain. The brain has different structures; the cortex, or the outermost part, which processes complex thinking abilities like speech, memory, spatial awareness, and even personality. On the other hand, the inner parts take care of the fundamental aspects of being human, like emotions, fear, and impulses. While the subcortex allows the transmission and processing of information.

Focusing on the latter part, our subcortex processes information through input, storage, and output systems. Starting with input, once our brain is exposed to a particular stimulus, it immediately examines and gauges the information. Then, our brain automatically stores this information by mentally "encoding" it. Finally, the brain decides what to do with the information and how it should react to the stimulus.

The brain is so powerful that it constantly processes and analyzes all thinking patterns. Since it's built to process a mountain of information, how come we sometimes lose control over our thoughts? The more relevant question is: what clutters our brains?

1. *Information Overload*

Stress is one of the main reasons humans feel pressured by life's difficulties. Stress, by definition, is "a state of mental or emotional strain." When stress piles up, it triggers various mental issues like anxiety, depression, panic attacks, and overthinking. Coupled with physical symptoms like sleep problems, headaches, and even intestinal disorders, your brain becomes burdened with concerns that paralyze it from being able to differentiate and prioritize legitimate issues—a glaring sign of information overload.

Since the brain continuously processes information daily, the probability of information overload is high. We're more at risk if we add our quick access to technology, instant information, and entertainment one click of a button away. When we fill our brains with streams of anything and everything, it creates an illusion that each one of these is essential and urgent. But still, we are unable to immediately declutter thoughts and information because we make ourselves believe that we are "too busy." Ironically, we are just too busy gathering more information.

We fail to realize this: the more information we consume, the more our brains succumb to mental and emotional exhaustion. This is because we receive, store, and react to stimuli endlessly until our breaking point, which causes mental fatigue. Hence, when the brain is exhausted, it has a hard time processing information, let alone thinking, focusing, and reasoning.

2. *Choice Overload*   (solution commitment.)

Renowned psychologist, Barry Schwartz, coined the term "paradox of choice," or the phenomenon of having so many choices that it overwhelms you. While choice overload seems like a privilege, it is starting to be a problem in the modern world.

As the world has become more innovative over the years, the world offers a broader array of options. This pertains to anything from universities to enroll at to the brand of fresh milk to purchase. However, now that we have more choices, psychology reveals that we also have a more challenging time deciding which option is the best.

Under the paradox of choice, our freedom becomes more limited by having too many choices because "unlimited" possibilities are harder to grasp and even harder to satisfy. Instead of the concept of more choices bearing increased benefits, it can have lesser returns in terms of mental health. Simply put, more choices equate to higher levels of anxiety, indecisiveness, and dissatisfaction, which adds to the clutter in your head that needs "fixing."

An example could be a multiple-choice exam. If the answer to a question is limited only to four choices, you have a 25% chance of getting the correct answer. But if options were increased to ten choices, the odds of getting the right answer decrease to 10%. The same applies to the paradox of choice, where being overloaded with options has more disadvantages in easing your mind. By choosing only one answer out of ten, one is left to wonder what if the correct answer is in those remaining nine. Thus, instead of feeling rewarded by making a choice, we feel more burdened with the other choices we didn't make.

The thought of "what-if" or "I should have" intensifies with the number of choices available. In turn, it only worsens the state of your mental clutter.

3. *Negativity Overload*

It is believed that our ancestors, starting 600 million years ago, have passed down a particular trait to all of us: the tendency to react more strongly to a negative stimulus than a positive one. By virtue of self-preservation, the human brain evolved in a manner where we overestimate threats, according to Dr. Rick Hanson of UC Berkeley. From here, the negativity bias was born.

We can blame this trait on why our brain activity increases dramatically in the presence of a negative stimulus. Our brain reacts more intensely and quickly when it comes to threats. Because of this, our brain goes on an override of overthinking, worrying, and creating imagined scenarios that make problem-solving more difficult. By now, we all know how these negative thoughts impact our overall mental and emotional ability. As the mind goes haywire with negativity, it scatters more unnecessary thoughts into our minds, further clouding our judgment and our decision-making skills.

With more accessible information, more options to choose from, and more threats to ward off, our brains become more vulnerable to continue running without a proper course of action as their destination.

As our thoughts multiply, it becomes more challenging to identify how to declutter one after another, especially when each one appeals to you with urgency. The concept of being mindful of your thoughts sounds a little bit too simple for a solution, but mindfulness is something that can be practiced and perfected. Like all habits, decluttering the mind is one that requires the resolve to take the first step until walking through it feels natural.

Section 10: Effective Ways to Declutter Your Mind

Nothing else is more distracting than a room full of clutter. How can you start your work if a pile of clothes has invaded your chair? Clean or used, you can never tell them apart. How can you rest for your afternoon nap if the smell of your breakfast still lingers in the room? I mean after you forgot to bring out your dirty dishes. How can you relax if your room has litter scattered on the floor? An allergy-triggering amount of dog fur on the furniture? A bunch of unpacked items from your trip last month? And things you should've fixed during the weekend if only you didn't keep saying, "I'll do it tomorrow?"

You may think you're saving time and energy by ignoring these things and dealing with other "important" matters. Still, these things bother you throughout your work, studies, and even relaxation, causing more pressure and stress. A cluttered mind significantly uses more time and energy than physically cleaning things up. The good news is, cleaning a room full of clutter only requires a broom, maybe a vacuum, and a mop. But cleaning a cluttered mind requires patience, willpower, and healthy thinking patterns.

So, let's go through simple and effective ways to declutter your mind.

1. *Declutter your physical environment*

Stimulus in your room or home makes your brain feel stressed and anxious. The need to constantly remind you to clean, tidy up, and organize is preventing you from focusing on just one thing. As a result, your brain is distracted, and so are you. According to the Journal of Neuroscience, a cluttered environment causes chaos in your head as these external factors compete for your attention, which restrains your ability to process information correctly and accurately.

At the moment, cleaning may feel overwhelming, especially if you've made yourself a schedule you want to stick to. But in mental decluttering, starting small is a great tip to get you moving. For example, you can start by organizing a drawer or a cabinet. Start from there and continue the progress, no matter how slow. At times like this, it's important to remind yourself that one of the brain's functions is to respond to its environment. So, if its environment is cluttered, it will react to it suitably...and not in a good way.

2. *Sleep, relax, meditate.*

When it comes to your mental fitness, sleep is the best remedy. The correlation between sleep and psychology has long been established. For example, most people with mental health problems also suffer from sleep problems like insomnia. So, what is the most common piece of advice? Sleep well.

Since the mind functions non-stop during our waking hours, allowing it to rest—through getting enough sleep—enables it to think straight, remember better, and make wise decisions. Hence, your brain's general ability is maintained or improved with proper rest. On the other hand, temporary mental lapses or "brain fog" occurs when a person is sleep deprived. This is because your brain cells communicate with each other poorly when the brain itself is exhausted.

Besides sleep, your brain can be rewarded through meditation and other relaxation techniques. The restorative intention of meditation is to reset the brain by inducing mental clarity.

Creating a mental refuge wherever you are and no matter what you're doing allows you to destress and achieve a state of rest and peace. Furthermore, meditation also has long-term benefits when practiced religiously. These benefits include a developed sense of well-being and empathy, an improved ability to focus and make decisions, a sharper memory, reduced physical and emotional pain, and even a state of enlightenment.

3. *Start a journal*

If your mind is burdened with many things, like random thoughts, creative ideas, grocery lists, meetings, appointments, or a mental to-do list, relieve your mind by writing it down. Empty your mind by storing these disruptive thoughts elsewhere. It could be a paper, a small notebook, or even a journal. Keep it close and write down the things you want to remember later or just want to unload. This idea allows you to separate the thoughts that can be dealt with later.

Apart from this, journaling your thoughts and feelings can also help alleviate the chaos inside your head. With a journal, you can scribble your plans for the future, creative business ideas, things that cause you worries and anxieties, inner monologues, and even conversations you wish you could have with someone. Journaling is an excellent form of writing that allows you to ponder your problems and maybe even devise a solution. You can clear up room in your mind by emptying all these onto a page.

4. *Set priorities*

When we're overwhelmed with several things to do, we're most likely unable to comprehend where to begin—especially when everything feels urgent and vital. When our brain tries to process different things at once, we feel clueless and stuck. The inability to identify priorities would send us into a panicked frenzy if we weren't already there, to begin with. So, take a moment to list all the things you need to do and then identify which ones need confronting now and which ones can be set aside for later.

By reminding ourselves that not everything has to be completed simultaneously, we lessen the things that need worrying and focusing on. The more we pressure ourselves into meeting one deadline for everything, the more negative impact it has on our mental ability; it slows down our information processing and decision-making. This is why it's relevant—and even life-changing—to learn how to prioritize. Prioritizing helps you clear your mind and stay organized. So, set aside the mental clutter and focus on the must-dos for the day.

5. *Limit information intake*

Since information overload is one of the modern culprits of a cluttered mind, reducing information intake is the simplest way to relieve the brain. These days, our brains swim around in a sheer volume of information from news, television, emails, text messages, and social media that we're close to "drowning." Indeed, the internet has expedited research and data gathering, but it also made mental fatigue come in quicker.

Singer Bo Burnham was correct when he said, on the internet, "anything that brain of yours can think of can be found." Since the internet can satisfy our curiosities and entertain us to cure our boredom, we fail to realize that the internet has also directed us to senseless and unnecessary usage. We can take a quiz to find out which Disney character we are or what kind of fruit we are based on our personality, but for what? For no apparent reason.

Our minds can be bombarded with useless sensory facts much easier now, adding and storing irrelevant thoughts in our brains, like a snail can sleep for three years and women blink more times than men. Hence, we must be disciplined when using our devices and the internet. When we read less useless information and watch less unhealthy shows, we allow our minds to take a break from processing knowledge we'll never use in our lifetime. So, go through your inbox, unsubscribe from websites, blogs, and newsletters you don't read, block spam messages, deactivate social media accounts if possible, and avoid aimless internet browsing. Monitoring our information intake decreases triggers of negative thoughts and feelings and, ultimately, reduces the clutter in our heads.

6. *Be confident, be decisive.*

Under Abraham Maslow's hierarchy of needs, we are wired to achieve a sense of belongingness—even if we have to earn it by compromising our comforts and boundaries. Unfortunately, for some people, the fear of being disliked or rejected is so intense that they're willing to go beyond personal ethics to impress others. When this happens, commitments and appointments tend to overlap to the point that your schedule becomes overwhelming.

In reality, we cannot do everything; some things we commit to are not even necessary in our lives. Thus, we must learn not to feel obligated by every request, favor, or invitation. There is power in saying "no." If your boss requests you to work an extra hour, but you're already tired, politely say no. If a friend asks a favor you're not comfortable doing, don't do it. If the social event you've been invited to has no significance in your life whatsoever, don't attend. Only engage in things that are worth your energy and your time. Only do things that are good for your mental health.

Because we overthink what other people would feel about us if we say no, we begin to develop unrealistic work and life expectations. But once you say no, say it confidently and be firm about it. After all, you're saying no to reduce the weight of your already cluttered mind.

The truth is that the clutter in our minds is the unarranged collection of information, emotions, experiences, and fears that our brain reacts to daily. It is impliedly expected for all of us to learn how to weed out useless information from important ones. But it is also up to us to act on them or keep them for tomorrow's agenda.

Except, when we set aside certain things, we must develop the habit of coming back to work on them—no matter what. Don't let mental clutter pile up that it feels like hard work.

Section 11: The Best Relaxation Techniques You Can Use

Between sleep and other forms of cognitive rest, the former gets the most attention and credit when it comes to the question, "how can you keep your brain functioning well?" Indeed, a complete eight hours of sleep for an adult is what scientists recommend. Similarly, the solution to the panic, the hurry, the demands, and the mental clutter that wears and tears your brain is the opposite of being productive—being idle.

Thankfully, the human body is naturally equipped with the ability to rest and relax to balance out and fight off mental fatigue. What needs more recognition is the other type of cognitive rest, and it's called relaxation. Yes, it's the ability to stay at ease while disengaging yourself from a task that requires too much attention. However, "disengaging" and "being idle" are often misinterpreted as laying on the bed, eating potato chips, and watching bad trash

TV, but that's not what relaxation it's about; it's about stimulating your body's natural relaxation response. Below are some techniques that might work best for you:

1. *Deep breathing & muscle relaxation*

    Deep breathing is the most straightforward and powerful relaxation technique. Apart from the fact that it doesn't ask too much from you, it's usually the first step to submerging your mind into a state of rest. From controlling panic attacks to meditating, deep breathing exercises help calm one's nerves by introducing a wave of calmness into your body, starting from your lungs. Deep breathing can be done whenever and wherever; thus, it's the fastest way to reduce stress levels and hit the pause button on a cluttered mind.

    With deep breathing, you can either sit comfortably or lay on your back. Then, inhale through your nose and exhale through your mouth; feel your muscles tighten and relax; this is called progressive muscle relaxation. Now, keep count—even if you only do it ten times every time you feel overwhelmed.

    While at it, allow your breathing to control the strained muscles in your body. As your muscles ease, let your mind do the same. Recognize how stress accompanies physical symptoms like back pain and muscle spasms. Allow your mind and your body to relax.

2. *Meditation & visualization*

    Meditation is a popular technique to achieve a state of calm, even more so with regular practice. It trains a person's awareness and attention to incorporate a healthier sense of perspective. In layman's terms, it's momentarily turning off your feelings and thoughts.

    One of the forms of meditation is called body scan meditation. Like progressive muscle relaxation, it requires you to divert your attention to certain parts of your body, feeling how each body part feels, starting from your feet to the top of your head. Instead of tensing and easing the muscles, you feel the sensations in your body—tune in with these sensations.

    Since every technique is unique, finding the right one that works for you matters. So, you can also try mindfulness meditation. Before beginning this exercise, we must answer, "what is mindfulness?" Mindfulness is not letting the worries of the past rob you of today's happiness. It's living in the moment.

    Mindfulness meditation requires putting your attention on repetitive actions like breathing or mantras. It can even be physical activities like walking and exercising. The most important thing when doing this is constantly returning to the present. When we listen to ourselves think, our minds often wander to the bitterness of the past; this is when we have to be mindful and quickly come back to the gratitude of the present. When we get the hang of it, we create a more powerful mental habit of not allowing guilt and regrets to affect us.

If these forms of meditation aren't the right fit for you, guided imagery or visualization, as extensively discussed earlier, is another technique you can try. Basically, visualization is creating a scene in your head to calm you. For example, you can imagine sitting on the beach, the sand getting in between the spaces of your toes, the sound of waves colliding with the shore, and even the breeze that kisses your skin. Perhaps, you can be on top of a mountain, overlooking nature beneath you, the sun over your head. Allow the same mind that troubles you to soothe you. Allow your senses to indulge in this imaginary reprieve.

As taught in the previous chapter, remember to feel your breathing, feel your body, and freely float inside your mind. Hear your woes, converse with yourself without judgment, and then validate these thoughts—not because you're powerless over them, but because forgiveness can only come after acceptance. Release yourself from the weight of living, but return to it. Only this time, you're returning with a clearer head. With overthinking and mental clutter, visualization lets you momentarily step out of life when it becomes too much. Like a short vacation, every hard worker deserves one.

3. *Movement, exercise, yoga*

Movement and exercise are scientifically proven to reduce the body's stress levels. It activates the production of endorphins, known as the body's natural mood regulator and painkillers. Thus, rhythmic movement and exercise are also other methods. You can walk, jog, run, hike, dance, and even swim. To elevate this, you can also incorporate mindfulness into the mix to engage yourself in the moment as you exercise. While you do these, feel the body's movement and recognize the sensation. If you're swimming, appreciate the lawless gravity when submerged or feel the temperature of the water. Your breathing, senses, and body should all work together to achieve calmness of the mind.

Yoga also combines breathing and movement to reduce stress and anxiety. Learn this better by watching video instructions, attending classes, or hiring private instructors. Since there are different variations of yoga, you can start with Satyananda, which is most suitable for beginners. You can also try Hatha yoga which is gentle for learning the basics, and power yoga which is more intense but equally relaxing.

These relaxation techniques require regular practice to maximize their stress-relieving benefits. However, it doesn't have to be demanding or time-consuming if you are busy; doing it once or twice daily is already enough. Furthermore, understanding that these techniques do not immediately relieve you from the clutters of your mind is necessary. Like all habits, gradually immersing yourself in practice and making it a part of your lifestyle takes time.

| Part 2 | Mastering Your Emotions

Section 1: What Are Emotions

Feelings and emotions are words that are often interchangeable, if not synonymous. So, what's the difference between feelings and emotions, and why are emotions vital in understanding the self? Well, first, feelings are subjective; it's a reaction from personal experiences *and* emotions. On the other hand, emotions are triggered subconsciously; it's a psychological state—as natural as instinct and intuition. While feelings require the presence of emotions, emotions don't need feelings to be generated. It's an innate ability. Since emotions dictate how to respond to stimuli, it also allows us to identify how we should feel about a situation. Psychology has summarized the five main reasons why emotions are important: it helps us take action, survive, strike and avoid danger, make decisions, and understand others. Of course, just as we can use it to understand ourselves.

We all have seven basic emotions: joy, sadness, surprise, contempt, disgust, and anger. Researchers established two dimensions of analysis when analyzing these emotions: arousal and valence. Arousal is the psychological state of being conscious, able to react to stimuli, and processing information, but it cannot determine the quality of these emotions; hence, valence addresses whether the emotion is positive or negative.

Geared with this newly-acquired knowledge, we delve deeper into how emotions affect us. In its truest sense, emotions have exclusive power over our thoughts. Being an unconscious trigger, it lays down the "groundwork" for us to feel and act appropriately. Our emotions initially trigger urgent behavioral responses, especially when there is no time for us to think things through. Emotions support our decisions and motivate us to take the appropriate action. To illustrate, before you can feel fear, your emotions have already communicated with your nervous system, causing your muscles to tense and even your heart rate to go faster. From here, it is you, however, who makes the conscious decision on what to do next.

But of course, our emotions may be unconscious, but how we respond to them impacts our lives more than we know. So, when making decisions, the best tip is to make a decision on an equal plane between emotion and logic. When your emotions are heightened, your logic is diminished—and we tend to make irrational decisions with poor reasoning. For example, when you're too excited, you overestimate your odds of succeeding and underestimate the risks. When you're too anxious, you may overgeneralize and allow one worry to seep through other aspects of your life, like getting sick would lead to you missing a class, failing the subject, not finishing the course, not graduating, and then ultimately, not getting a job. When you're too sad, you set lower expectations for yourself, hindering you from reaching your full potential. Finally, when you're feeling intense emotions, like anger and embarrassment, you make high-risk, low-pay-off decisions.

Knowing your emotions alone is not enough to get you through the ups and downs of life, but knowing how emotions play an important role in decision-making can. Balanced choices require us to acknowledge emotions and raise our logic to decrease emotional reactions.

Your emotions don't simply process stimuli and interact with your nervous system, it also plays a significant role in your quality of thinking and overall living.

Man, by nature, is insatiable—he is not easily contented. From money, relations, properties, and all other worldly possession a person can own, he desires it. Some desire it. Perhaps it's because the modern world has provided us with more things to acquire; different brands of phones, clothes, shoes, and many more. It's an abundant world. But if the world is so abundant, how come people still feel like they lack something? Why do they want more? It may be because of the phenomenon of *hedonic adaptation*.

Hedonic adaptation or hedonic treadmill is the tendency of people to return to a stationary baseline of happiness rather quickly. This means that regardless of a positive or negative event taking place in our lives, our level of happiness (or sadness) will ultimately stabilize again or come back to where it's emotionally neutral. Although people have different baselines of satisfaction, hedonic adaptation confirms that we all return to our baseline. For example, let's say you won the lottery. You feel ecstatic, lucky, and grateful when you find out having won the lottery. You think you can conquer the world. As a result, your happiness level increases dramatically. It can also apply to grief. If you recently lost a friend, you are thrown into feelings of devastation and despair. Maybe you'd even feel you can never recover from the loss. But the theory of hedonic adaptation indicates that, in time, you will recover from these situations and return to your "normal" baseline of happiness. Either euphoria or wrath, you are bound to regain emotional equilibrium—the ability to adapt to our current situations is a part of human nature.

For a lot of people, the high that comes with acquiring new things or a better social status is what drives them to want more. Hence, some people believe that having more is equivalent to becoming happier. But with hedonic adaptation, we'll come back down from the high, sooner or later. Failing to realize that this is the way of life and, instead, seeking more is what makes people seem insatiable. The pursuit of happiness appears to be a continuous struggle, but the real battle is the failure to see what truly matters in life. The truth is happiness is not equal to materialistic items. Happiness is being content with your life—your purpose, your well-being, and even the love you give and receive.

1. *Meaningful relationships*

   A study from Harvard revealed that among 700 people, meaningful relationships result in a happier life. Unlike what we often misconstrue, it isn't money, fame, or status—it's good relationships. Indeed, the journey to finding happiness is easier with a companion.

   Humans are social animals, and we genuinely crave spending time with people we love and care for. Hence, we are scientifically happier when surrounded by family, friends, and significant others. Under the concept of social happiness, people who openly engage with more people are happier; if anything, love and friendship are among the most rewarding experiences of our lives. To test this study, if someone asks you to close your eyes right now and think of the happiest memory you have, you'll most certainly recall a memory you shared with someone else. Why? Because as evidenced by history itself, familial love, friendships, and commitment contribute to happiness and well-being.

2. *Purpose in life*

Another essential factor for happiness is the sense of purpose in life. Tracking four years of research revealed that people with a higher sense of purpose have better physical health, reduced anxiety, less pain, and significant happiness.

Purpose in life answers the ultimate question of "why?". Why do we wake up each day? Why do we do what we do? It gives reason to our decisions, work, and relationships. Finding a purpose in life, and living by it while enjoying it, is a critical factor to a happy, content life.

3. *Good health*

One of the most important things we take for granted is our health. Sometimes, when we say "enjoy life," we interpret it as eating to our heart's desire—unhealthy foods included. We drink, smoke, and party constantly with our friends. We also skip a few hours of sleep, thinking it's okay, and we barely get any exercise. But one of the keys to a happy life is a healthy body, physically and mentally. Although happiness feels like an internal ordeal, for the most part, the mental cultivation of happiness also translates externally, meaning a healthier body. Psychology even tells you that you must be mentally well to be physically well, and mental wellness is strongly associated with happiness.

While we're young, living a healthy lifestyle doesn't feel that urgent, but it's one element that truly matters in life. So, eat healthy, stay hydrated, exercise, rest well, and keep track of a healthy body and mind.

4. *Self-love and self-acceptance*

Many people already know this, but not many live by it: loving and accepting yourself is where true happiness lies. Our biology may demand us to seek love and acceptance from the people around us, but the secret to a positive life is really within us.

As cliché as it sounds, you have to love yourself first before you can truly love somebody else. How? By accepting your flaws, everybody has them, and that's what makes everyone human. By forgiving yourself because mistakes are meant to be made and learned from. By looking at the world with optimism and letting go of grudges that wears out the beauty in living. By appreciating your growth and progress, no matter how long it takes.

"It all starts with yourself," remember that—make it a mantra if you must.

But research can only tell us so much about what matters in life, but it's up to us to live fully and happily. Then again, there's no harm in building good relationships, finding your purpose in life, keeping healthy, and embracing who you are. The truth is, happiness doesn't have to be as theoretical as finding your baseline—instead, find contentment. So pay attention to what counts in life.

Section 3: How To Use the Wheel of Life to Your Advantage

If living is what we make it, why do we make it complicated? The hard truth is that most of us feel slightly exhausted with life. Maybe a little anxious, a little depressed, and a little stressed. So relaxing can sometimes feel juvenile that even in our quiet moments, we still find our minds drifting back to our worries as if we aren't entitled to peace. We worry about everything—our career, family and friends, money, and intimate relationships. We worry about the things around us, our faith, our immersion in society, and even our health. The things to do while you're alive is a long list. All these worries have already been made into a diagram, and it's called The Wheel of Life.

The Wheel of Life represents various aspects of our lives that we must juggle and balance. Below is the visual made by a life coach, Paul Meyer:

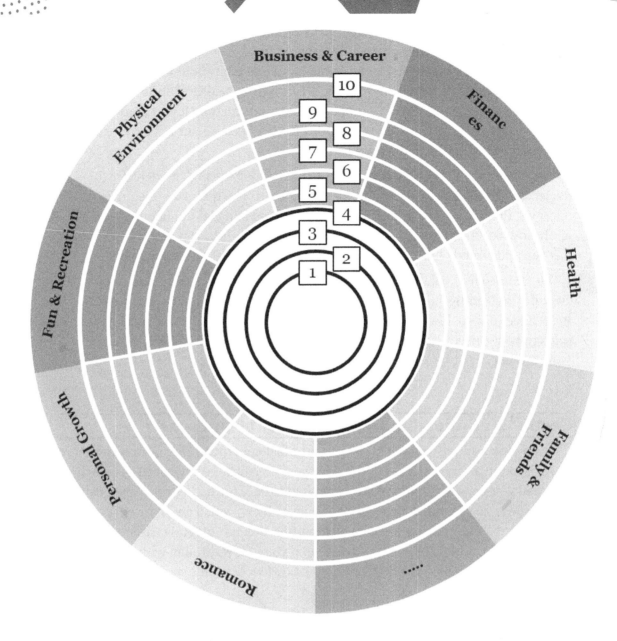

As illustrated in this diagram, the aspects of life may seem demanding, but all these are equally important for a happier life. Understanding The Wheel of Life is basic and upfront; using the aspects on the wheel, rate your level of satisfaction in each area, one being the lowest and ten being the highest. Map the data you rated for each and see if you created a perfect circle—as what it's supposed to look like, ideally. If it isn't equally distributed, like the diagram presented herein, identify which aspect you are most dissatisfied with and start working from there. Find a solution to why you are not as satisfied in other aspects of your life. After all, this diagram was intended to identify where your life has gotten out of balance.

Let's say a particular person is significantly successful in her career. She also has a happy family life and a supportive partner. She has adequate money in the bank to cover her needs, wants, and even emergencies. Some would say she is happy and well-off. But she takes several medicines before bed to make up for her deteriorating health—antidepressants, sleeping pills, and other supplements. She's a workaholic; she finds no time for recreation and relaxation. In fact, she's starting to feel stuck with her life. It's because she's led an unbalanced life and neglected some aspects of the wheel.

It would be best to view the wheel as your entire life. Through it, identify which aspect you've neglected and which you gave your most energy to. The thing about equally distributing your energy is that it's vital to acquiring self-satisfaction and general happiness in life. But why do all these aspects have to be balanced? Simple, because how can a wheel run smoothly if a part has been neglected? Like a car, one malfunctioning wheel can cause a crash.

The main goal of balancing the wheel is related to contentment and happiness: it's feeling "whole." Becoming "whole" includes a healthy body, mind, and spirit. So, identify the imbalance in your life and then work on satisfying yourself more on that aspect. It doesn't have to be a perfect wheel so long as the difference is insignificant. Nonetheless, you'll find your center.

Section 4: Understanding Your Why or Purpose

If you look around you, the happiest and most contented persons out there are those who have found their life's purpose. Ever since you were little, you've been asked what you want to be when you grow up. You probably even had a diary for listing your "life goals." By 18, you'd start college. By 22, you'd have your dream job. By 25, you'd get married. 27, you'll have kids. And so on. Life seems easy—when you are little. But, as you grow wiser and older, you realize that life doesn't unfold as you wanted. Even if you follow through with your goals, something's missing. You probably asked yourself, once or twice, what's my purpose in life? But before that, what is purpose?

Call it an awakening, if you will, but your purpose in life is what makes you feel like a better person; it's something that fulfills you and makes you feel whole. It's the driving force that gets you out of bed and keeps you on your toes. That thing makes you feel your blood pumping—it's passion. You may not have uncovered it yet, but your purpose has probably been already set since the day you were born, and deep down, you already have the answer; you just have to dig a little more. So, how?

Successful people learn the fastest way to find your purpose: by knowing yourself more intimately. If you dive deeper into the essence of who you are, chances are, you'll discover what you truly want to do with your life. To start it off, ask yourself: "why do I need to know my purpose in life?" Understanding why you need to find your purpose is key to understanding your purpose itself. Although it sounds complicated and borderline philosophical, a[...] purpose gives your life—your whole existence—meaning. Life without a purpose i[...] monotonous, unsatisfying, and incomplete. It's a life that will lead you to a path fil[...] with fears, worries, anxieties, and unhappiness. You may not know this, but the people who have found their purpose unlocked new talents and skills in the process. They learned about new strengths and weaknesses. Ultimately, knowing themselves better made accepting and improving themselves easier.

Now that we've established the importance of finding your purpose, the next step is to find it. Your personal treasure hunt begins now, and the reward will make your life fulfilling and your existence a legacy. Here is a guide to finding and understanding your purpose:

1. *Reintroduce yourself...to you*

In finding your purpose, knowing yourself is crucial—this is why you must converse with yourself again. Reintroduce yourself to you- this means learning different things about yourself, including your beliefs, "demons," dislikes, and passions. Have an inner conversation with yourself and identify these things.

First, identify your beliefs. In the search for purpose, one rarely notices that their beliefs sometimes get in the way. Perhaps, years of struggles and self-doubt have instilled in you the thoughts that you can't do it, or your efforts will be futile. Maybe when you're beginning a project, you are stopped by your wrong belief that you are incapable. It's similar to your so-called "demons" or the tiny voice in your head that whispers harsh things to you, like you'll never find your purpose or you don't deserve a purpose at all. Although hearing these thoughts is complex, you must acknowledge them; that is the first step to fighting them. When you listen to this voice to prove it wrong, it loses its power over you. What follows after is telling yourself kinder words of encouragement. Sow thoughts that you can do it and that you're worth having a purpose—most notably, reap it.

The second thing you must identify is your dislikes, discomforts, and the things that physically and mentally drain you. Point out the tasks that don't necessarily bring you happiness, and stop doing them because engaging in purposeless activities will drain your physical and mental energy. Now that you seek your life purpose, you must choose wisely which activities deserve your energy.

Your passion is another essential factor to identify. Why? Because your passion is highly likely related to your purpose. There is a reason why doing what you're passionate about doesn't feel like hard work—you take pleasure in doing it. If you haven't found your passions yet, it's time to start exploring the countless things you can be passionate about. You can start small by reading a book, watching an environmental documentary, learning to bake, and joining an art class. Perhaps you have a knack for writing, love wildlife, or have a hidden Van Gogh within you. Find what you enjoy doing, what you're eager about. Your purpose is hidden somewhere in your passions.

2. *Narrate your story*

In reintroducing yourself, re-telling your story comes hand-in-hand. Remind yourself of the challenges you conquered, the lessons you gained from them, and the experiences that made you stronger. The narrative doesn't need a happy ending; it just has to be raw, honest, and sincere. Our experiences will help us make sense of ourselves even better.

A 2008 study found out that the meaning and purpose of life lies within the change and growth you've experienced, so looking back at your story helps you retrace this growth. This reflective process is essential to unlocking your sense of purpose. If it's not in your passion, it must be in your story and journey. It is no coincidence that popular motivational speakers have used their stories to inspire others; they just happened to realize that their purpose is to inspire with their life stories. Who knows? Maybe your story is your purpose.

3. *Envision the life you desire*

To further understand and appreciate your purpose in life, it's time to visualize the life you truly desire. Close your eyes and imagine that future; what are you doing? Who are you with? Are you happy and fulfilled? Of course, you are—that's the life you deserve. It will echo in your everyday life if you believe you deserve it. You'll be one step closer to fulfilling your life's purpose. You see, your purpose isn't just about what you're doing but also how you're feeling while you're doing it. Accomplishing your purpose is as fulfilling as the definition of the word gets. It's even more fulfilling when you're doing it with other people.

In the life you're envisioning, also imagine the community around you. Imagine your family members, friends, social circle, and even support groups in the mix because our sense of purpose can sometimes be found in the people around us. So, find the right community for you. The good news is you've probably already started. Our purpose often reflects on our company; it could be within our parents, siblings, friends, and significant others. Reflect on how they impact your life and how you impact theirs; if the answer is on a positive note, your community is leading you closer to your purpose.

4. *Define priorities, eliminate distractions*

"Live your life to the fullest," they say. But how can one live a whole life if one lives with other people's expectations, impossible standards, and false objectives? The world seems like an active landmine, trying to sabotage you from succeeding in finding your purpose. So, define true priorities in your life. It's probably not the bad habits you've developed throughout the years or the unnecessary schedules you have with your peers. Even the demands of society shouldn't make the cut. These are nothing but distractions.

Although it's easier said than done, building the confidence to live your life the way you should live it according to your priorities helps you focus more on what truly matters.

5. *Cultivate gratitude and generosity*

It's already well-documented that positive emotions promote better physical health and mental well-being. Some positive emotions you should incorporate into your life are appreciation and altruism.

Several studies have revealed that cultivating appreciation and awe makes us feel more connected to something bigger than ourselves, perhaps, the world in general. In effect, we feel inspired to give back to the world. These emotions build a tremendous foundation for finding our purpose—gratitude and generosity. At this point, we already know that giving back is associated with a meaningful life. Gratitude and generosity represent the infamous "give-and-take" advice. We give something, like kindness, and take another in return, like the rewarding feeling of purpose.

Relative to this, it is essential to thank the people you gain inspiration from—the people who fueled your drive to keep going also deserves the credit. Just as great relationships give life meaning, gratitude to them strengthens this relationship.

Understanding your life's purpose is one long journey ahead. At some points, the journey would feel exhausting and pointless, but it's guaranteed to be worth it. Your purpose is not just something to ease your boredom from living; it gives meaning to it. Finding it will open up new experiences, opportunities, and possibilities. This could be your legacy—the very breadth of your existence.

Section 5: How To Find Your Ikigai

Ikigai is a word with a sweet aftertaste, but what's even sweeter is the meaning of this Japanese word. When the concept and definition of Ikigai were first mentioned in 1996, it only gained popularity from thereon. Today, its interpretation couldn't be any more precise; Ikigai is the highest level of human desire, but it's not just any desire—it's the universal human experience. It is more than biological and social satisfaction. As some would say, it's the desire to become "spiritual beings."

But being "spiritual" isn't exactly being religious. In Ikigai, being spiritual is bringing the essence of your consciousness into the world and transforming it. It's the reconciliation of your internal and external purpose; when introduced fully to the world, the imagination and comprehension of the human mind allow one to fulfill the highest sense of purpose. The thing about humans is our main program is survival; satisfaction is only secondary. Still, satisfaction or fulfillment has significant importance in our life. So, we often ask what's our meaning and purpose. To be spiritual, you must fully welcome your consciousness into the world. After all, humans are meant to be conscious beings--more than just self-preserving. This evolution is an inevitable impulse of the universe.

Japanese dictionaries define Ikigai as "something to live for," "the joy of life," and "the goal of living." Some terms relative to this also translate to "a life worth living." Generally, it's the reason for living a meaningful and purposeful life.

Ikigai is also a diagram that helps you find wondrous things about yourself, the same wonders you can share. The Ikigai diagram looks like this:

This four-circle diagram represents the relationship of humans with the world itself; a soft reminder that the world made us, so we should make it. There is a reason why the circles in Ikigai overlap with each other: it's because they should. Many people would argue that the real purpose in life lies in giving back to the world. To fully immerse yourself in this life-changing culture, here are the ten rules of Ikigai:

1. Keep in Motion & Stay Active
2. Do not go too fast
3. Avoid overeating
4. Have a circle of good and positive friends
5. Aim at being fit and healthy for your coming birthday
6. Laugh and smile a lot
7. Connect with the environment and nature
8. Be thankful
9. Live in the present
10. Follow your Ikigai

Ikigai may feel like an overwhelming way of living, especially with its rules, but your life's purpose does not have to be extraordinary or grand. It can be straightforward—as long as it makes you genuinely happy. Your Ikigai, as a matter of fact, can be as simple as afternoon coffees with your parents, a light drink with your friends, or even a quick stroll around nature. You may wonder how something so ordinary can be an Ikigai. I mean, how can that answer the needs of the world? But you see, Ikigai is not about career or money. It's not about changing the world; it's creating a life well-lived and allowing that fulfillment to echo to the people coming after you—Ikigai is personal and reflective. Your Ikigai can be multiple things at once. As long you enjoy it, it makes you happy and gives your life a sense of purpose; you should pursue it.

Section 6: What Affects Your Emotional State

Emotions are subjective. By definition, it is something that can be influenced by stimuli occurring around us, like thoughts, memories, experiences, and anything that our senses can register in our brains. It may seem like a simple reaction to events, but emotions affect our well-being scientifically. But apart from scientists, philosophers also pondered about emotions; how can something subjective cloud a person's judgment or make one impulsive? The ultimate question is if emotions influence us to the point of causing us more harm than good, why can't a person just function purely on logic?

Unlike logic, emotions are easier to recognize by persons. Since time immemorial, emotions have relied on specific survival strategies—from sensing danger to running toward safety. Emotions don't just make us impulsive; it's been aiding us throughout life. It gives our lives meaning. Even better, our emotional state can change our life.

A healthy and positive emotional state can help us achieve our "peak state," or the state of rising beyond the past and adopting a perspective of excellence—to inspire others to do the same. But before we reach this holy grail of mental state, we must refuse the mediocrity in our emotions and use it to our advantage, if not master it. Since emotions are a by-product of physiology, it is easily influenced. Thus, we must learn to control it through emotional mastery.

Emotional mastery is changing our subjective experience or controlling our reactions to events we have no control over. For example, if traffic usually makes you impatient and agitated, change how you feel because you have no control over the traffic. If the weather usually makes you sad, appreciate the weather instead. If you feel like arguing with an important person in your life, urge yourself to hug them instead. We can develop positive emotions by concentrating on them. By incorporating these ten "power emotions" in our daily lives, we create the condition to feel good about ourselves. These emotions are gratitude, passion, love, hunger, curiosity, confidence, flexibility, cheerfulness, vigor, and a sense of contribution.

To further achieve the peak state, we must also understand the triad of emotional psychology by Tony Robbins, where three elements must be mastered to control emotions: physiology, focus, and language.

1. *Physiology*

    Physiological psychology refers to the study of how human behavior and perception are affected by neurological functions. Since physiology dictates how we should feel based on the stimulus around us, we must recognize how our bodies and emotions are interconnected. This concept also dictates that we must take care of ourselves. Intuitively, we know getting that getting enough sleep improves cognitive function, and eating healthy improves memory and mood. While having good posture makes us calmer and more confident—as proven by Amy Cuddy's research on power poses, discussed previously.

    Keeping your physiology healthy is easier than you think; small acts make a big difference in maintaining or improving it. Start with getting enough sleep, preferably between 7-9 hours a day. Drink more water, at least two liters a day. Eat more unprocessed foods. Reduce sugar intake. Get physical, as in exercise every single day. Go out briefly for fresh air and sunlight. Take multivitamins and supplements. Manage your stress. You see, your physiology isn't asking you for too much; it just requires you to be healthy, so the mind can perform better.

2. *Focus*

    Place your focus where your intention lies—that's where your energy should flow. By focusing on the things you are working toward than things weighing you down, you divert your attention to the positives in your life. This is an essential step in achieving your peak state. By not letting your fears trample on your vision, you welcome a healthier mindset on top of a healthier body. Remember, the driving force that controls our life begins with focus.

    Some strategies help improve focus, like practicing mindfulness or diverting your attention to the present, cognitive training or improving attention and response time over a significant period of time, and acquiring a healthier lifestyle.

3. *Language*

To stay on track with a positive perspective and a focused mind, you must be mindful of your language or how you talk to yourself. Always choose wise and kind words when speaking to yourself. Your internal dialogue shapes how you behave in the world. If you find yourself speaking in a negative direction, replace it with a positive one. If you find yourself tongue-tied over them, seek help from family, friends, or co-workers. Once you get used to speaking encouragingly, your internal voice improves. As such, your language plays a role in changing your focus and achieving your peak state.

So, how do you improve your inner dialogue? First, stop whenever a negative thought pops into your mind; don't allow yourself to bring yourself down. Second, ask yourself questions—so your brain starts to seek answers and call for action. Third, talk to yourself in the first person; it's not "you," it's "I." Lastly, motivate yourself; incorporate statements like "keep going," "you're doing so well," and "I'm proud of you" every now and then.

Mastering your emotions can do much for your growth as an individual—it improves your relationships, makes you more productive, and helps you achieve your goals and visions. So, take care of yourself, shift your energy to where it matters, and speak to yourself with kindness; all these will teach you the art of consciously reshaping your life experience for the better.

Section 7: The Power Of Focus

Nothing is more powerful than perfecting the "Art of Focus." This concept may seem short-sighted, but your achievements and future may depend on your ability to focus. Apart from our drive, focus also gives us a sense of purpose—the fuel that keeps us from moving forward. But since we're only human, we often get caught on focusing on the negative aspects of life. Just as your focus can kickstart a great future, it can also squash your hopes for the present; but only if you allow your mind to get caught in that trap. So, what should you focus on? The things that matter.

Focus on what you can control

Some things don't always go the way it's planned, and when that happens, we often find ourselves drifting into thoughts that we have no power over, like what awful thing will happen next? When we do such, we end up sulking and worrying so much that we feel helpless. Neuropsychology dictates that thoughts create emotions; our thoughts trigger the link to our emotions—this is why thinking negatively results in pessimistic emotions. This is why we must focus on what we can control.

In focusing on what you can control, you must divert your thoughts to things within your control. Redundant but straightforward. The task is to identify and separate things that are in your control and are not. For example, if your partner was having a bad day and unintentionally raised his voice at you, should you feel bad and blame yourself for not being more considerate? No. Why? Because the thing is, you have no control over your partner's situation and reaction—but you have control over yours. So, for the sake of maintaining a "sunshine state of mind," don't blame yourself and don't think you didn't do enough; think that you did nothing wrong and that his sour mood will pass.

Remember, you are the driver of your life—you have control. Therefore, intentionally choosing a positive attitude is a sign of being rational and emotionally mature. Even better, it makes you optimistic and motivated.

Focus on what you have

There is no problem with wishful thinking; hoping to buy or acquire something is anything but human nature. But letting these thoughts run wild to the point of jealousy and self-hatred is the problem. These negative thoughts distract you from what is important: what you have.

In life, somebody will always have it better than you—the bigger house, the better car, the latest bag, shoes, or clothes, and that's just the way it is. If we allow everything to bother us because we don't have it, we will strive to have everything, regardless of what it means on a personal level. It doesn't only waste our money and resources but also our energy and our happiness. Jealousy and dissatisfaction will only rob us of our joy; thus, we must focus on what we have. Not just focus on it but also appreciate it.

What you have doesn't necessarily pertain to material things; it can be a skill you developed or want to develop. It can be a friend or a person you want to befriend—and become friends with in the future. It can be a unique or new experience; how about trying to cliff dive? Attending a music festival? Baking your cake? Riding a hot air balloon? And if you hate moving around too much, maybe you should try staying in a new city; a cozy surfer's shack by the beach, or a floral-scented countryside. These are some experiences you can have.

Although there is no formula for happiness, studies show that satisfaction accounts for 50% of a person's happiness. By focusing on what you have, you conjure satisfaction in your life. If you think about it, you are halfway through acquiring complete happiness. Isn't that the better thought than "why don't I have this and that?"

Focus on what you can do

The hard truth is that we impose restrictions and limitations on ourselves because of anxiety, depression, or even our physical capabilities. For example, anxiety may tell you, "you may get the answer wrong, don't recite." Depression may say, "why bother yourself going to work if you're destined to fail anyway?" Your physical health may even wholly restrict you from doing something, like asthma stopping you from becoming the field and track competitor you always aspired to be. It's so easy focusing on things we can't do. But how about we focus on what we can do?

Aristotle once said, "the whole is greater than the sum of its parts." The same applies to you; don't deduce yourself to parts that "work" well and parts that don't. You are more than the things you can't do. In fact, you are more with things you can do. So if your physical health doesn't allow you to engage in athletics, be grateful that you are still capable of doing other things. Perhaps you were meant to be in the bedroom writing songs.

Focusing on what you can do is appreciating your personality, style, humor, interests, intelligence, and more. Then, give yourself credit for your capabilities—that's how you change your mindset for the better.

Balance your focus between past, present, future

"Living in the present moment creates the experience of eternity." Author Deepak Chopra said. Although the concept of mindfulness has been stirring the field of psychology these days, the key to happiness doesn't solely rely on being in the present. New studies reveal that focusing on a balanced perspective on the past, present, and future can make you happier.

The San Francisco State University demonstrated that a balanced perspective on our timeframes could make us stronger, more graceful, and more satisfied with our lives. Why? Because focusing on the past is recognizing your history or getting stuck in it. Focusing on the present makes you comfortable with the "right now," but forget the valuable lessons of yesterday. Focusing on the future is to anticipate what's yet to come and steal away precious moments of today. The thing is, focusing on only one of these timeframes can make your life go out of balance. To find out if you're out of balance, ask these questions:

"Is my past hindering me from embracing the present?"

"Is my present a problem for my goals in the future?"

"Is my future making me lose sight of my past?"

If you answered in the affirmative to these questions, your life is unbalanced. So, the tip is to balance all three timelines together. You must learn from the past, enjoy the present, and prepare for your goals in the future. Don't let one timeframe overshadow another; create a clearer picture of your entire life.

Focus on What you need

There are just one too many things in this world that we can all indulge in; traveling halfway across the world isn't as tricky as it was back when horses took us places. In fact, if we want a particular delicacy a few hours' drive from us, we can just order it and wait for it to be delivered to our doorstep. But, unfortunately, in the modern world, almost everything is a finger's touch away, and this accessibility, although convenient, has groomed us to be insatiable.

Insatiability is the enemy of contentment. With so many things we can possess, the urge to have them all is a hard thing to battle—that's why it's time to recenter your focus: focus only on what you need. Why? Because the only thing stopping you from happiness and satisfaction is your insistent earthly desire to gain more—even when it's unnecessary. Never lose sight of the essentials and the necessities; after all, it keeps you alive. What you need is what you should prioritize.

Focus on What's Good

It's hard not to think that sometimes, our minds are the villains, often discouraging us, making us question our worth, and reminding us of things we didn't mainly succeed in. It does a great job of showering us with discouraging thoughts. But, although it often fails to motivate us, we must never forget that we have more control over our mind than our mind does over us.

Focusing on what's good in your life is a great way to quash self-doubt, anxiety, and procrastination. By now, we've established that bad thoughts are the root cause of our inefficiency and unhappiness, so why let them dictate what we can and can't do? Nothing is more empowering than seeing and appreciating the good things in our lives.

If you're familiar with the saying, "you attract what you are," then you know that being a pessimist will only attract negativity. Depressing thoughts only lets you notice the bad in everything. Say your new dress has an almost invisible tear at the sleeve, and you worry that someone might see it and criticize you—like you notice this one bad thing because your mind tells you to. But if you focus on what's good, you'll notice that your new dress looks good on you, has the right fit, and the color complements your skin. The good and the bad are always lurking around you. And in the battle of choosing between them, seek the good in everything. Redirect your focus on what's good—attract the good because that's who you are.

Focus on Where you are going to go, not on your fear

Author Roy T. Bennett said: "Focus on your goals, not your fear." But these words are more than just literature and encouragement; they echoed and changed the lives of people everywhere, including surfing athlete Layne Beachley, who witnessed firsthand that fear sabotages the dreams of some of the world's athletes.

If skilled and experienced athletes succumb to fear, who are we to think we can rise above it? But that's precisely the thought that prevents us from success: fear and self-doubt. When confidence chips away, the reason is set aside, the effort is ignored, and achievement becomes further—hence, the lesson everyone should learn is to focus on where you're going—your goals and aspirations. Empowering yourself with positive emotions keeps you on the right track and directs you toward optimal results. Becoming aware of your potential is the antidote to fear that often limits us.

It isn't unusual advice, but focusing on the things that matter can change your life. We often fall short of appreciating life because we focus on the wrong things—things that hamper our potential to succeed and become happy. By reminding ourselves to focus on the right things, we teach ourselves to love our life more.

Section 8: Strategies To Direct Your Focus and the Use of Empowering Questions

Although your brain is the most intelligent system in your body, literally, it only adopts and acts upon experiences that influence your decision-making. Exquisitely, the brain is designed in such a way that it learns from harsh and painful memories and then stores them as a way to protect you should a similar situation arise. To some extent, your brain probably focuses too much on the threat, danger, fear, and all things negative, thinking it is a way to save you from re-experiencing difficult situations. But incessantly focusing on the negative can hamper your ability to live a happy, optimistic life.

Sometimes, a person becomes so used to unfortunate experiences that they become pessimists or even develop the so-called phenomenon of learned helplessness. This is where they no longer attempt to improve their situations because they believe the result would be pointless, as it has been. Since success is based on chasing opportunities, it takes inner fortitude to jump after them. If one thinks of failure, he conjures failure. Hence, one must direct his focus towards a positive attitude to increase the odds of finding success and happiness through these three steps:

1. *Part ways with the negative you*

    If you let yourself focus on the negative things, you'll live a life plagued with persistent doubt that will affect your choices. In reality, submitting yourself to the cycle of skepticism will make succeeding difficult, if not impossible. The remedy? Part ways with the negativity in you—focus on the positive things instead. It may sound repetitive, but consciously and actively centering your life on things that make you happy will stop you from constantly limiting your potential. This thinking approach allows you to connect with the reality of who you are and the possibilities of who you can be.

    Cutting off ties with your pessimism is one way to calm your mind and relieve yourself from the chaos, stress, and distraction it brings to your mind. So, exhale deeply and let go of your negative thoughts. What you need in life is a refresher.

2. Train your brain

Now that you've cut "communication" with your negative alter ego, it's time to unlearn the pessimism it taught you. How? By retraining your brain to focus and perceive the positive things happening around you. Of course, negative situations can't be avoided, but one way to recover quickly from them is to find silver linings. Things happen for a reason—even in bad things; so find a reasonable explanation for why it's happening. Most likely, there's a lesson you're supposed to learn that is crucial for your personal growth.

When it comes to thinking patterns, paying attention to how you process thoughts is essential. If you become aware of how negative you are, you become more conscious of avoiding it or changing it completely. As soon as the negative thinking kicks in, turn away. Between anxiety and confidence, always choose the latter. Sticking to new habits is as crucial as slipping out of old habits. Allow yourself to learn a healthier thinking pattern.

While the brain may have the unhealthy habit of emphasizing bad things, you must actively scan for good in everything. A simple tip is to write down three positive things that happened to you during the day; regardless if you think it was a bad day, focus on the little wins.

3. Pay the positivity forward

The third step to directing to a positive focus is the most rewarding one: engage in acts of kindness to make others feel good. You may think this has nothing to do with you, but acts of kindness actually play a role in boosting our happiness. Doing something nice is a great way to break the negative cycle. Now that you're a little happier and more optimistic pay it forward. Do a favor for somebody. Donate a dollar to an orphanage. Give food to a homeless person. Compliment a stranger. These small acts that make people smile reinforce positive feelings in you—instantly. By incorporating this daily, you make yourself happy every day.

But apart from daily acts of kindness, you have to be in the moment every day—focus on "now." Develop the habit of mindfulness. Ask yourself, "what am I thankful for in this moment?" "What can I do right now that will give me joy?" "Can I do something for someone right now to make them smile?" These questions only concern you today.

So, you've directed your focus into the positive light of life; what's next? Well, it's time to learn a new critical life skill that will improve the quality of your life: asking yourself empowering questions.

You may not notice it, but the mind loves it when you ask questions; it systematically curates an answer based on your memories, experiences, feelings, and thinking patterns. However, some questions can distract us—only if we allow them. This time, we're asking questions that direct our focus. We are asking ourselves empowering questions. But what are empowering questions? These are questions that can direct our focus to possible solutions and transform our state of mind into thoughts that help us move forward. Some examples of empowering questions you should ask yourself often are as follows:

1. What is the smartest way I can solve problems?
2. What are the benefits of my current situation?
3. What do I love most about myself?
4. What things do I excel at?
5. What gets me excited about life?
6. What will my success look like?
7. What motivates me to become better each day?
8. What do I want to do with my life?
9. What's the most effective way for me to keep moving forward?
10. What are the lessons I can learn from this setback?
11. What are my values in life?
12. What other opportunities can I pursue?
13. What can I do right now that will help me succeed?
14. What can I do to overcome my fears?
15. What are my short-term and long-term goals?

Don't these questions sound so much better than disempowering ones? But, of course, disempowering questions should be avoided since they only give you stress and anxiety. Some examples of these negative-fueled questions are as follows:

1. Why do I perform or work poorly?
2. Why do I suck at my new hobby?
3. Why am I so unlucky?
4. Why do people seem not to like me?
5. Why can't I be fit, tall, or have perfect skin?

The most obvious reason for avoiding these questions is that thinking the worst will only make you feel worse. Most of these questions leave you with the impression that you are lacking in some ways or incapable of doing something altogether. Asking your mind "why" with a negative premise is a way to depreciate your self-worth, and it's a practice that results in poor mental fitness. So, why do it?

Right now, asking yourself empowering questions may seem to have little effect on you. But by including it in your lifestyle, you improve your quality of life—as the questions you now ask yourself are ones that empower you, direct you to the possibilities of life, and, ultimately, help you succeed in life.

Section 9: How Your Physiology Affects Your Emotional State

If it still isn't apparent to you, the mind and the body are connected in ways more than one; our physiology is a link to our emotions, and vice-versa. Thanks to years of countless studies, we have established a direct correlation between the brain and the body, where the communication network exists throughout every nerve. The actual scientific concept that the mind controls the body is no longer just science anymore; it is also psychological. It isn't also just a one-way concept of brain-to-body, but also body-to-brain. How? Through matter and mind.

Matter is a synonym for the body and the mind for the brain. Experts have revealed that emotions are the nexus of mind and matter. It turns out our emotions are also cellular signals transmitting, processing, and translating information that can influence both receiving ends in no particular order. This means that your body can trigger your emotion first and then communicate to the brain. The most conventional example of this is our so-called "gut feel." It is no coincidence that we can feel "emotions" deep in our guts. The weird sensation in your stomach you initially feel triggers emotions. To break the myth, our intestinal tract is an emotional receptor causing us to develop gut-related instincts or "butterflies"—these are products of emotional reasoning alongside intuition. Your body felt it first before your brain translated it.

The relevance of this information falls on the new reality that our physiology affects our emotional state. If the food we eat can affect our mood, who's the say our posture cannot? Thus, we return to the recently discovered link between our posture and mood. To illustrate, pay attention to your posture when you're sad—your neck, back, and shoulders are slumped while your head is turned downward. Of course, one would argue that you're seated that way because you're sad, but science can also say that you're sad because you're seated that way. Yes, this is the new study of embodied cognition.

In cognitive science, embodied cognition is the study that unveils that the mind is not only connected to the body by nerves but that the body also influences the mind. At the genesis of this concept, Amy Cuddy sought the opportunity to impart to us the beauty of "power poses." The idea is by displaying confidence, we feel confident.

It seems shallow to say that feeling tall can improve our mood, but it has already been proven that our posture can tell our brain that we are powerful. And a little bit of self-encouragement goes a long way. Further research fueled this concept, wherein sitting upright allows a person to think of empowering thoughts and traits much easier than those in collapsed positions. This is because your posture is a means of elevating your energy levels—the higher your energy levels, the happier you are.

So, researchers now share a straightforward way to improve your emotional state: spend two minutes positioning your body in a "power pose." Straighten your back, push out your chest, and hold your chin higher. Improve your mood through this simple action. To remember it, set an alarm daily and commit to it. You can also incorporate good posture in your daily activities, like raising your rearview mirror when driving or increasing the height of your study table.

Suppose you have wondered why more people are depressed in the modern era. In that case, one of the causes is that the people of today spend so much time on their desks, computers, or phones to the point that it disrupts their posture, later affecting their energy levels and overall emotional state. So, instead of becoming another number in these statistics, start incorporating "power poses" in your daily life.

Section 10: How To Control Your State To Your Advantage

Emotions impair decision-making—this is a fact known to and proven by science. As an example, if you are happy, you make goal-driven decisions. If you are excited, you are more willing to do things. If you are sad, you tend to settle because you feel helpless. If you are angry, you make rash and impulsive decisions. If you are afraid, you take longer to make decisions. As you can see, your emotions can make you develop poor judgment, recklessness, unconscious bias, and risk aversion; why this happens is no coincidence but purely science.

Most of the time, emotions are triggered when the brain interprets its surroundings. By understanding the role of emotions in our decision-making process, we can find the perfect balance between intuition and reason. So, how do we control, or say, override, our emotional state to our advantage? This is how:

1. *Take Responsibility*

    Often, we find ourselves blaming someone or something when things go wrong. Blame traffic for being late to work, blame your roommate for the messy living room, blame your upbringing for your temper and intolerance—and we all do it. But because we shift the blame elsewhere but ourselves, we get to a point where we convince ourselves nothing is wrong with us and things just happen as they should, including how we feel towards situations surrounding us.

    When we let ourselves believe negative emotions are something that we can't do anything about, we allow the negativity to consume us; to manifest in our bodies, like increased muscle tension, a racing heartbeat, or even an upset stomach. We enable self-doubt and hatred to make us sadder or more anxious—all because we believe there's nothing we can do about it. But there is: taking responsibility for your emotions.

    True, there are some things you can't control, but you can control how you feel about everything. Although it's easier to blame something or somebody else for our sadness or disappointment, we must keep emphasizing to ourselves that we are the only ones with absolute control over our lives, our emotions included. So instead of allowing our emotions to lead us to a corner of helplessness, let yourself help you. To take responsibility for your emotions means to take responsibility for your life.

2. *Do Rhythmic Breathing*

    Breathing exercises can do wonders in regulating emotions. Physical symptoms, like an increased heart rate, can determine our physiological state. One of the simplest ways to steer your emotions is by becoming aware of your physiological state and controlling them from overwhelming you.

As soon as the physical symptoms of stress begin, don't allow yourself to dive into that chaos and choose to achieve a coherent state of mind by breathing exercises. Research shows that deep breathing exercises increase oxygen supply to the brain, stimulating the body's parasympathetic nerves and, in turn, promoting calmness in your state of mind.

3. *Choose Your Emotion*

If you don't know it yet, we have over 34,000 emotional states. Although, understandably so, most of us can only identify several emotions, ranging from anger, anxiety, fear, happiness, excitement, and satisfaction, to name a few.

So, what's the next step now that you've practiced rhythmic breathing? Choosing the right emotional state for whatever situation you're in. By default, our brains already know what emotion to trigger based on memories and experiences, but if we fail to properly express our emotions, our brain will only choose between the fight-or-flight state; neither of which is actively doing anything to help us—it's either we overreact or not react at all. The thing is, there is a right emotion for everything; you just have to choose correctly. This practice can help alleviate stress and even make you wiser when it comes to making decisions.

4. *Practice Awareness*

Being aware of the multitude of emotional states isn't enough; you must be able to utilize this awareness to your advantage. Awareness entails that you can tell apart which emotion you're feeling—excitement or nervousness. Maybe acceptance or indifference.

Emotional intelligence is vital to enable yourself to act appropriately during your highs and lows. Emotions and logic should come into play before committing to a particular action. Knowing how emotions work and affect our behavior is merely a theory. If we cannot apply it to our daily lives, find the appropriate emotion to manage your response. Manage your response to make better decisions.

5. *Change Your Feelings*

The actual peak performance of using your emotional state to your advantage is being able to change your negative emotion into a positive one. Since being emotional impairs our judgment and thinking abilities, allow your emotions to change from hopelessness to determination or anxiety to calmness.

It is no secret that negative emotions affect us the most. But we don't notice the same thing goes for positive emotions. It can influence your mindset, your behavior, and even the people around you, all through positive reinforcement. Remember, decisions are always better with a clear mind.

The real lesson is to look at both opposites of the spectrum of emotions—even the in-betweens. Emotions don't always have to be associated with anger, sadness, disgust, or fear; also, notice happiness, satisfaction, and calmness. With 34,000 emotional states to choose from, surely, we can pick the ones that give us the taste of pleasure in living.

Section 11: Adopt Empowering Words To Improve Your Emotions

Would you believe it if a wise stranger told you that you could change your life by changing your vocabulary? How about shaping your destiny by consciously choosing the words you attach to your experiences? If it seems new or absurd to you, it's time to learn about transformational vocabulary.

Although we may think words are intended for communication, it's so much more powerful than that, especially now that psychology has proven that words can create your vision or prevent you from your goals. With transformational vocabulary, we use the power of words to transform our feelings. Yes, words can affect your emotional state more than you pay attention to. So, before we delve further into this subject, ask yourself this first: do you communicate with yourself in an empowering manner? Think about the answer as we proceed.

The brain may seem complicated with all its different parts and functions, but it's easily trained, so much so that repeated thinking patterns can become conceived beliefs. Before you know it, your thoughts have controlled your life with flawed beliefs. For example, constantly using the word "can't" deflates your hopes each time. Saying "I can't do this" or "I can't be successful" can prevent you from acting towards your goals. Do it repeatedly, and you may just completely lose hope. But what happens if you change the word "can't" to "must?" Say, "I must do this" and "I must be successful"—just one word changes the meaning and the tone of the entire sentence. It takes one word to change self-defeat to self-encouragement. This is transformational vocabulary.

Empowering words are what make transformational vocabulary revolutionary. Using the right words can elevate your emotion, improve your perspective, and change your life. Now, pay attention to the disempowering statements below and their empowering counterparts:

"I hate the freckles on my face."
"I have yet to love the freckles on my face."

"Why am I always so emotional?"
"Have I always been this passionate?"

"I've been depressed for a year now."

"I've been working on myself for a year now."

In these examples, you can easily spot which statements are disempowering and which ones aren't. It's easy to identify them, especially since it uses words like "hate," "emotional," or "depressed"—words that are often associated with negative connotations. But if we use words like "love," "passionate," or "working on myself," we transform our negative emotions into something powerful. The right words can open up possibilities for improvement.

Besides turning negative statements into positive ones, we can also improve our vocabulary to make us feel better. For example, when someone asks you how your day was, instead of answering, "it was okay," say, "it has been incredible." Below are some more examples of improving your words:

"He is so funny."

"He is so hilarious."

"That dog is so cute."

"That dog is adorable."

"Your sister is charming."

"Your sister is enchanting."

"Were you always this creative?"

"Were you always this artistic?"

"Our new co-worker is hardworking."

"Our new co-worker is zealous."

It may not seem hardly relevant, but choosing intensified words over mediocre words is one way to appreciate the simple pleasures in life. But then again, even the little things—like your choice of words—significantly impact our quality of life. As Robin Sharma said: "Words can inspire. And words can destroy. Choose yours well."

Now, we go back to the question: do you communicate with yourself in an empowering manner? If the answer is no, it's the perfect time to choose your words wisely. Make sure it inspires you.

Section 12: Assigning A Better Meaning

In an ideal world, life would be rainbows and butterflies. Maybe in an alternate universe, the most challenging problems we'll encounter are which designer bag would look better on my dress or which country I should spend my weekend in. But in the real world, rainbows are reflections from raindrops, and butterflies only live for approximately two weeks. In famous words, life is hard. What makes it harder is our unregulated emotions and our erroneous assigned meanings. So what does this pertain to? It simply states that our brains may have been assessing situations inaccurately and giving things improper meanings.

Since the brain is always running, it's always out to solve problems and give meaning to the things around us—the problem is, meaning is subjective and easily influenced by our thought patterns, developed coping mechanisms, and personal beliefs. Based on our memories and experience, we may interpret things differently and give them diverse meanings. It's almost philosophical: what is "meaning?" It's like asking if clouds are soft.

To understand "meanings" better, here's an illustration:

You're at a study hall, and the professor reads a line from the book you're currently discussing. He said, "she looked like a withered flower." Now, he asked all of you what the author wanted to say about this line. One of your classmates said, "the author is saying the protagonist is exhausted." Another answered, "the author meant that the protagonist isn't as youthful for someone in her prime." Then, another: "the author implies that the protagonist had poor posture." But the actual answer is actually straightforward: the character looked sad.

In this example, we quickly observe that there are different interpretations for one sentence. Depending on your perspective, meanings can differ from another person. But assigning better meanings is not about getting the same meaning. Instead, it intends to create a better experience associated with a feeling you gave meaning to. Thus, your assigned meaning is interrelated, just as your feelings are connected to an experience.

Since we attach meanings to all situations, we can either positively or negatively affect our day-to-day experiences. Therefore, to create better experiences, we must assign better meanings. Here are examples of some situations where you can give better meanings:

Your partner didn't call you back within an hour.

Negative meaning: He doesn't care about you.
Better meaning: He's probably busy with other important matters.

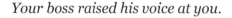

Your boss raised his voice at you.

Negative meaning: He doesn't like your work performance.
Better meaning: He is probably having a bad day and needs some time off.

You failed an exam.

Negative meaning: You are stupid.
Better meaning: You have to study harder next time.

Your friend didn't greet you on your birthday.

Negative meaning: She doesn't want to be friends with you anymore.
Better meaning: She probably forgot because she has other things to do today.

Your child got called to the principal's office.

Negative meaning: You are an irresponsible parent.
Better meaning: You get the opportunity to talk to your child if he has problems at school.

Assigning better meanings helps you feel good about yourself and the situations surrounding you. Unlike avoiding situations altogether, this technique lets you optimistically confront your problems. So, start with observing how you assign meanings to your emotions and then explore other possible meanings for them. If you can, assign new, better meanings to specific moments in your life. Think of this process as a domino: better meanings result in positive emotions, and positive emotions result in more extraordinary life experiences.

| Part 3 | Setting up the Bases for Growth

Section 1: Understanding Mindset and Paradigm

Paradigm and Mindset

In the literature of psychology and philosophy, a mindset is a fixed mental attitude or a habituated perspective. In other words, it's a tendency to think in certain ways that may be useful in some situations but detrimental in others. A paradigm, on the other hand, is a set of assumptions about life and reality underpinning one's goals and beliefs. It's basically an interpretation of your world with the purpose of making you feel secure and comfortable even if what you believe is incorrect or untrue.

These two concepts are related to each other, understanding this dynamic can help us improve our lives.

Paradigms act as blueprints for people's mindsets or the mental attitudes they hold towards life. Knowing this relationship can help us better understand why most of us are emotionally attached with certain beliefs and patterns in our lives whether we're aware of them or not . In addition, it can also help us choose what kind of paradigm we want to live by so we can truly become happier and more fulfilled.

So what are some paradigms that may be keeping us back from living the life we want? They include:

- Money is everything, having it will solve all your problems.

- Being rich (and beautiful) is better than being poor (and ordinary).

- Wealth brings success which leads to happiness.

- The best way to succeed in life is through competition. You need to beat others to get ahead of them.

- If you're not happy now then you never will be; this world isn't made for joy and pleasure. Happiness exists only if you really feel it.

- Without beauty, money, status, etc., there's no point in living.

If you believe most of these paradigms, then most likely your mindset is built upon them. And if you think about it closer, you'll realize why they may not be very helpful in making us feel better about ourselves or improving our lives. This doesn't mean that we shouldn't have any money or that competition isn't worth pursuing, rather it means that we should evaluate the beliefs and assumptions that guide us towards success. It's only when we achieve this balance between supporting our goals while maintaining healthy thinking that can we finally understand what it really means to live with purpose , compassion and confidence.

The importance of having a good mindset

A mindset is how we interact with and view the world around us. If you have good thoughts about your abilities, opportunities, and possibilities; we call this a growth or an opportunity mindset. If you feel that everything is hard and difficult; then this is called a fixed mindset or negative mindset.

The first step towards achieving something great in life is having a growth-oriented attitude where you seek out new challenges as opposed to avoiding them because of the fear of not being able to meet certain standards or some other reason. The second step is to have a learning-oriented outlook. If you are ready to learn from your mistakes, rather than being afraid of failure - then this is called as a growth mindset.

What are the benefits?

People with good mindsets tend to be more optimistic and enthusiastic. They see mistakes simply as opportunities for improvement, instead of something that makes them feel bad about themselves or inferior to others. People with good attitudes always give their best, even if they know that they might not win or succeed at first. This will motivate them to keep on trying and improve over time, which satisfies those around them as well. Furthermore, people with positive attitude understand that no matter who we are, we all make errors now and then; making mistakes is actually a very important part of life and we cannot be perfect all the time. When you believe that mistakes and failure are okay, it will greatly improve your confidence and motivation to try new things.

How can I get a good mindset?

First, accept the fact that positive thinking is not an easy thing to do - it takes practice! You need to remind yourself of this fact whenever you feel tired or discouraged at first. Second of all, you should understand that improving your attitude is a gradual process; so if someone said they got everything right on their first try then they were lying. Third, start with small goals; don't go for bigger goals if you haven't mastered the smaller ones yet. Once you master each step one by one, you will naturally start to enjoy the journey, and eventually your efforts will be recognized.

What should I do if I can't seem to control my negative thoughts?

Don't give up on yourself! Negative thinking is a bad habit that we all have sometimes, but it's not permanent. We all slip up from time to time, and that's fine. The trick is learning to get back on track as soon as possible. Every time you notice that you're thinking negatively, stop yourself and switch to positive thoughts. You can't completely ban negative thoughts from your mind; but if you actually pay attention, then it's much easier to stop the "negative" train of thought in its tracks before it goes too far.

Paradigm & the subconscious mind

The subconscious mind is the part of your brain that processes information about an experience, so you can make sense of it. It also tells you how to think and feel about what happened or might happen in the future. If you have an experience that is unpleasant or negative it will be stored in your subconscious mind.

The word paradigm comes from the ancient Greek language and means 'something that stands before. Paradigms are strategies, models, methods or theories used to give meaning to something. They are mental filters that determine how we see the world around us.

As with everything in life, people are motivated by different things. Different paradigms provide a sense of purpose for understanding the world around us. Each person has their own unique paradigm which is based on experiences, beliefs, attitudes, and values they have learned throughout life. Over time these paradigms become deep-seated ways of thinking about ourselves and our lives.

Your personal mindset is made up of beliefs, attitudes, and values that correspond to your paradigm. Your mindset influences the decisions you make as well as how you react to things in life.

The problem with paradigms & mindset

If our paradigms are too narrow this may cause us to miss opportunities or fail to take an alternative approach when a problem arises. For example, a person who thinks they should be able to complete every task on their own will struggle if they don't have all the skills required for a job. A person's mindset can also hold them back from trying something new or going into unfamiliar situations because they feel uncomfortable doing so. This can lead to people feeling stuck within their current situation and not being able to improve their lives. In addition, different ways of thinking can cause conflict between people as perspectives on life.

Change your paradigms and mindset for the better. A paradigm is a way of thinking that determines how you relate to the world around you. New paradigms allow different ways of thinking about things, which may lead to a change in behavior or action. When a person's paradigm changes it will influence their mindset and decisions making throughout their lives. It can also help them respond differently or handle situations more effectively because they have an alternative way of looking at problems. Changing your paradigms may take time but with effort, it is possible to develop new beliefs, attitudes, and values that make a difference in life.

How to change your paradigm and mindset

There are several ways to change your paradigms. The first step is to create awareness of your current paradigm so you can work out how it affects what you do. It's also important to think about the experiences that have contributed to the development of your personal beliefs, attitudes, and values. Once you understand what influences your thinking, choose new things that will help you grow as an individual. This may include learning new skills, meeting with people who share different views or taking up a hobby. Being more flexible in how you see things can give you opportunities for self-growth and enrichment in life which result in greater fulfillment. Why not try some of these ideas with friends or family members? It may give you something to do together while also helping you develop new ways of thinking about life.

Changing your paradigms is the first step towards reaching goals and improving your mindset. Developing new beliefs can help improve how you see yourself which will lead to better decisions in all aspects of life. When you feel more positive about yourself it's easier to find opportunities that will motivate and inspire you to become the person that you want to be. It is possible for anyone, regardless of age or background, to make changes in their lives if they are willing to put in the effort.

A positive mindset can help you achieve great things and make the most of life. By understanding your current perspective, creating awareness of how it affects what you do, and choosing new beliefs that will support your goals, it's possible to develop a positive paradigm and mindset. Changing paradigms may take time but investing in self-development is always worth it for increased happiness and motivation throughout life.

The law of attraction and the law of giving

The law of attraction and the law of giving are two sides of the same coin. You cannot have one without the other. The law of attraction is all about getting what you want, while the law of giving is all about giving what you want. Both laws are based on the principle that like attracts like. When you give, you attract more things to give to. And when you get, you attract more things to get. It's a never-ending cycle that will bring you happiness and abundance if you let it. The law of attraction states that like attracts like; the fundamental principle of all abundance. So when you get, it is because you are in alignment with the universe to receive more. When you give, it's because you are giving something that is in resonance with your true self. If you want to give what you really want to give, then start by asking yourself 'What do I truly want?' The answer lies within yourself, not outside. Once you discover what brings joy and happiness inside of your heart, then align this quality with your intention - make it an honest intention - and act on it no matter how small or big the step may be. You will be amazed at the abundance that will manifest for you.

The law of giving states that when you give more of what you want, then you attract more things to give to. It's a fundamental universal truth that is found in every culture and religion

of the world. From ancient wisdom, we have learned this law works - so why not use it? The simplest way of doing this is by simply being generous with your time, energy and money. When people do me favors or buy me lunch/dinner/gifts without any reason, I always pay them back with something bigger later on. Sometimes it may take weeks or years, but I always remember those who were generous toward me first. And once I am able to help others, I feel happy and grateful to be able to give back what they gave me. These are the people who matter the most in my life because they activated that law of giving inside of me.

You can't talk about abundance without mentioning generosity! At some point or another, we all want more out of life - whether it's money, resources, love, o satisfaction - but we can never get more than we give. The world runs on this subtle universal law: When you give more than you take and do so selflessly and with good intentions, then you attract an infinite stream of goodness into your life. So start by giving more of what you want. It can be in the form of time, money or energy (or all three), but make sure your intentions are pure and that it comes from the heart - not through obligation or self-judgment.

Using subconscious to your advantage

The subconscious mind is the most powerful tool available to men. When harnessed, it can do anything. You must understand and realize that your world is a product of your subconscious mind, and what it believes to be true for you. Understand the power of beliefs and how they affect your life. Know that beliefs are just opinions or thoughts that you keep thinking over and over again until they become the truth. And the truth is that beliefs are all that you will ever need to accomplish anything in life, whether it is wealth, happiness, or even spirituality.

The paradigm shift on how you view the world around you has everything to do with your mindset at any given moment. You can choose your own destiny by making decisions for yourself and not allowing outside circumstances to control you. That's easy to understand but harder to do when fear, anxiety, anger, and other emotions cloud your thinking process. If you're afraid of what could happen if someone tried something funny on you while walking on a dark street, then rational thought about these possibilities gets clouded by heightened emotions that create stress in the body which makes decision-making difficult because of fear-based thoughts. So, when you have a mindset that's clouded by the small picture, nothing good will come to you.

When other people think or do things that hurt you, it is usually because they are in a similar state of mind. They may be selfish and not care about how their actions affect others around them, but these people have problems themselves. They're just being themselves and the only way they know how to get what they want from life. It has nothing to do with you unless you make it personal and pay attention to them long enough for anything negative that might happen to register in your brain. This is where having a fixed mindset will help them control your circumstances while promoting an abundant mindset can bring many positive changes into your life.

An abundant mindset means that you believe in the endless possibilities of the universe and know that nothing is impossible to achieve. You should not think nor behave like someone who's poor, or lacking in some way because if you do, then opportunities will never come your way to change your current state of being. It may take time for you to be able to expand your mind but it can be done through diligent practice which allows you to develop new habits and constructive ways of thinking. Everything in this world works like a machine, including people; they go around seeking positivity and avoiding negativity in their lives until one day it becomes second nature to them, replacing old limiting beliefs with empowering ones that help them get what they want faster than ever before.

The power of positive thinking is not a myth. It works because the subconscious mind controls all your actions, which you can use to your advantage if you focus on what you want in life instead of what you don't want. This means focusing on the things that make you happy and not allowing others to dictate how you feel. If someone tries to hurt your feelings or insult you in some way, do not take it personally as they are probably having a bad day and taking their anger out on whoever happens to be around them at the time. Avoiding this type of negative energy will go a long way toward protecting yourself from those people who spend their lives looking for new ways to drag everyone else down with them.

Remember that everything starts inside and if you want to accomplish something great in your life, then the first thing that should be done is for you to think big. If it's money that you're after, start visualizing yourself already as a millionaire and know that through positive thinking and intelligent planning, anything is possible. You may say that it sounds like I'm telling people to put on rose-tinted glasses but that's not at all the case. Abundance of any kind, whether it is happiness, love, friendship or material things is a personal choice and can be achieved if you're willing to learn how to use your mind properly.

A fixed mindset will make you worry about things that may never come to pass while an abundant mindset can propel you to greatness if you learn how to control your thoughts and emotions. Having a positive outlook on life is not always easy, but it's the best way forward because no matter how negative people are, they're still going to die someday just like everyone else. If that day comes sooner than expected then what will be left of them after they go? Nothing but a pile of dust, while you on the other hand will be remembered for your happiness and good deeds. Make the most of what you have because living in the past or dwelling on negativity will not help anyone.

Positive thinking, visualization, and the law of attraction

In the power of positive thinking, mindset is a major factor in how you apply your thoughts and feelings. In a sense, it can be defined as how you see things. In a specific context, it is more commonly referred to as Paradigm, which means the manner in which one thinks about something.

In physics and chemistry, for example, paradigm refers to the idea of a model or an example that serves as a basis for discussion. Your mind has been conditioned in such a way that when someone says paradigm, you will immediately think in terms of the above definition in science and not in a social sense.

The basic idea behind the power of positive thinking is that if you think positively, you will get positive results. This seems to be borne out by experience – most people who are successful in life have a positive attitude and believe in themselves. When you visualize and imagine what you want, your mind is at work for you. You are trying to influence it so that it does what you want. There is a secret behind this: whatever we put our attention on grows in our life.

If we focus on problems and difficulties and think negatively about them, they will grow bigger and proliferate in our life. If we concentrate on the positive things around us and within us, we shall find more of these coming into manifestation in our lives. In other words, everything happens by virtue of one universal law – the Law of Attraction which states that like attracts like or as the Bible says "As a man thinks in his heart so is he." You create vibrations within your being which travel through the Universe until they encounter others who are on the same wavelength as you.   wavelength

This being so, if you are thinking positive thoughts about what you want to experience in your life, then those are the thoughts that will attract similar vibrations to themselves and encourage them to manifest in your life. As these vibrations meet each other, they merge with each other and form even bigger ones. Sooner or later, these big vibrations will find a way of creating circumstances that will lead to the manifestation of what you have been thinking about because it has come together with many others like itself.

The Law of Attraction is always at work whether we realize it or not – there are no exceptions because it is one universal law that encompasses all things big and small including the physical universe, the Earth, our lives, and thoughts. When you are thinking about something that you want to happen in your life and you feel positive about it, then that thought will be like a seed attracting other similar vibrations and helping them to grow in your life. On the other hand, when we think negatively about something we do not want to happen or experience then we would likewise be planting seeds that can manifest as undesirable things in our lives at some point in time.

One manner of utilizing this law is through daily affirmations where you state out loud (or write) what you want in life.

Visualization is a powerful tool for manifesting your desires as well. When you visualize what you want, you are putting yourself in the mindset of already having it. This helps to activate the Law of Attraction, which brings more of what you desire into your life.

To use visualization effectively, first get clear about what it is that you want. Be specific and have a clear picture in your mind of what the end result looks like. Then, begin to imagine yourself having already achieved that goal. See yourself living in the reality of having accomplished it. Feel the emotions that come with it – happiness, joy, satisfaction.

Imagine yourself as if you already have it. Take as much time as you want to visualize this feeling, bringing it into greater and greater detail.

If you can't see the result clearly just yet, that's okay. It may take some practice before you are able to picture it in perfect detail. You can return to your visualization anytime for further work on it – just be sure not to overwork your brain by constantly thinking about the same thing! Instead, allow enough time between mental rehearsals so that they remain effective.

Remember – have fun with this! See yourself going through life with your goal already accomplished, experiencing all of the positive emotions that come with it. And that's how to put yourself in the mindset of already having what you want...

Section 2: Know Who you Are

It's important to know who you are and what you want in life. But how do we figure out who we are? We must first take an honest look at ourselves and our talents, strengths, interests, likes or dislikes. When we have done this then we need to make some decisions about where to go from here with these thoughts in mind.

People tend not to live up to their full potential unless they have a deep sense of self-awareness. If you don't know who you are, you're unlikely to be able to articulate what you want out of life (and thus unlikely to get it). And even if you do manage to get what you want, how will you know whether or not it really makes you happy? Is there anything better than knowing that your life is exactly what you wanted it to be?

Most people never really figure out who they are. They go through life wearing masks, pretending to be someone they're not. They do this because they don't know who they are and they're afraid of what other people will think if they find out. But the truth is, it's a lot easier to be yourself than to try to be someone else. And once you figure out who you are, you'll stop trying to be someone you're not and you'll start being happier and more successful because you'll finally be living your authentic life.

You can't ever achieve your true happiness if you don't know yourself well enough. We should all take control of our lives and find out who we truly are instead of existing as a carbon copy of ourselves; thus living an uninspired, insincere, and unfulfilled life. So go ahead and take the first step; determine who you are before you're overtaken by events and unable to do anything about it.

There are a few reasons why it's important to know who you are. First, it makes you happier and more successful. When you're living an authentic life, based on your own values and principles, you're much more likely to be happy and successful than when you're trying to live someone else's life. Second, it gives you control over your life. You're the only one who can change who you are, and once you know who you are, you can start making changes that will improve your life. Third, it makes you stronger. Knowing who you are gives you the courage to stand up for yourself and to make your own decisions, even when they're unpopular or difficult. Finally, it allows you to connect with other people. People are naturally drawn to those who are authentic because authenticity is something that's naturally attractive.

When you don't know who you are, people sense it right away and they'll start treating you differently. You won't be able to make decisions for yourself or stand up for yourself because you're not sure what the right decision should be. And when other people give you feedback about your behavior, rather than taking it as helpful criticism, you'll feel hurt and misunderstood because on some level you realize that their perception of you is different from how you perceive yourself. This will also prevent others from connecting with you because they'll see that there's a lack of genuineness in your interactions.

So remember strive to always be yourself. Don't try to be someone you're not, because sooner or later the real you will show up and people won't like what they see. But if they get to know the real you from the start, then there's a good chance that they'll appreciate your honesty and genuineness—two things that are very attractive in people.

What can you do to help the discovery of yourself

In order to find out who you really are, it's important to know what your values and interests are. The first step is understanding ourselves and figuring out what makes us happy. It might sound like a cliché, but happiness comes from within and if we believe in ourselves then anything is possible. The following steps can help you through the process

1) Identify your values and principles Write down a list of what's important to you in life, i.e., your personal values. Then write down a list of the principles that guide the decisions you make, i.e. your beliefs.

2) Identify your areas of interest, think about the activities that you really enjoy doing. How much time do they require? What skills are involved in them? Do you think that these kinds of activities could become a profession for you one day, or even a hobby? Once you have compiled this list, sort it in order from the most pleasurable activities to the least pleasurable.

3) Pick one activity that is most important to you When it comes right down to it, what activity or goal do you enjoy the most? This will be your priority. Make sure this goal fits in with your values and principles.

If you have trouble deciding on a priority ask yourself these questions:

What would I do if time was not an issue, money was not an issue, and I was guaranteed to succeed?

Which activity would I choose if I had one day left to live?

What do I spend most of my time doing when left to myself?

4) Think of the advantages and disadvantages Think about what you have to gain from achieving this priority. What would success look like? On the other hand, what are the disadvantages of choosing this goal?

5) Write a list of action steps once you have identified your priority, a list of small steps that will help you reach your goal.

Get to Know your strengths and weaknesses

Understanding your strengths and weaknesses is one of the most important things you can do for yourself. It will help you make better decisions about what to pursue in life, how to promote yourself, and who to hang out with. Knowing your strong points will also give you confidence when facing challenges that require those talents. And knowing your weak spots will keep them from holding back your accomplishments or sabotaging relationships that are important to you. You just need to be honest with yourself about the realities of who you are right now so that later on in life, it's not a surprise when somebody tells you what they really think about something because it won't hurt as much if it's coming from someone who knows how good or bad at something they think you are.

The importance of knowing your values and living by them.

It's no secret that we all have values that we live by. Some people like to joke, "No one is perfect," but this couldn't be more wrong. We all strive to live a life full of integrity and honesty; everyone wants what they do and say to reflect their beliefs and morality. However, it can feel overwhelming when you get down to the nitty-gritty detail of figuring out what your values really are. While the principles of living by your values seem simple enough, the task of defining them can leave you with a lot of questions.

Living by your own set of values is an important step in becoming a better version of yourself. It not only gives you a sense of pride, but it also allows you to have a sense of direction for the future. What are your values? Who are you? What do you stand for? How do you want to be remembered? These are all questions that we ask ourselves as we try to figure out our true selves, and it's a good thing that we do because it can be very helpful to define who you really are.

The process of defining your values can be simple. You just have to figure out what you stand for. It could be something as simple as, "I care for others." Share your values with friends and family to see if they resonate with you. Do you feel confident when you say your values? If not, it's important to keep finding other ones. The goal is to find values that are in alignment with you and with the people you care about. The following steps can help you through the process:

- Figure out what you stand for

- Share your values with friends and family to see if they resonate

- Do you feel confident when you say your values? If not, keep looking

- Find values that are in alignment with you and the people you care about.

What your values are is very subjective. It can be hard to figure it out when there is no wrong or right answer. In general, however, most people have at least a few shared values such as being kind, caring, and honest. These values are important because they're the foundation of your interactions with the people around you and they can help you to have a clearer direction for your life. It's good to surround yourself with people that share these values, but it's crucial to make sure that those people reflect the things you value as well as yourself. In contrast, it's important to stay away from people that reflect any negative qualities of your values. Negative examples can teach us a lot about who we are and who we want to be, so it's good to take note of them, but it is important not to emulate those traits because you could lose sight of yourself in the process. Your time is valuable and it's important to make the most out of it. By knowing your values, you can avoid people that aren't worth your time and energy.

Once you've found your values, it's important to remember them and live by them. This can feel like a daunting task at first, but there are ways that you can make this process easier. One way is to keep a list of your top five or ten values on hand at all times. For example Integrity, Honor, Respectfulness, Optimism, and Leadership would be a good list for someone who cares about his/her personal reputation. This way it is easier to remember them in moments of conflict or when you're making decisions.

Be confident in yourself and your abilities

Too often people tend to be ignorant of the things that they are good at. Oftentimes people are more concerned about the things they lack rather than all that they have done right. A common example is when an individual fails to complete a project assigned by their work, yet still receives praise from their boss for everything that went well.

If you are not confident in yourself or your abilities, take some time out of your day to recognize all the things you have accomplished. Write them down if you must, but do not overlook something as simple as a small achievement because you are too busy dwelling on your flaws.

Being confident in yourself is important for every aspect of life. This is applicable to your school, work, relationships, future career choices, and just about anything else.

Do not let others put you down.

Be yourself, but remember who you are.

You are great in your own ways, have faith in yourself!

If you do these things, know that when the time comes to prove your worth no one will be able to stop you. The world may seem full of cruelty when confidence is lost, but once it is found it can spread like wildfire and burn brighter than the sun. So do not give into sadness or despair because all hope is never lost until death ushers you away from this earth for good. Always hold onto what makes you happy even if it means letting go of something else. Nothing in life stays the same forever so cherish each with love and live life to the fullest!

You are capable of anything you put your mind to, so do not let the opinions of others influence how you feel about yourself. Be confident in who you are and never be afraid to speak up even if things seem bleak. You only live once so make the best out of everything you do. Be proud of what you have done!

Who are the people that surround you and how do they affect you

It's never easy to live in a world full of people. People are judgmental, quick to anger and slow to forgive. Each person has their own uniqueness that makes them who they are, but it also gives them different ways how they can see things. The way they think can affect the way you think as well. They can help you learn new things and can teach you more about the world. But this all comes at a cost. Each person in their own way affects who you are in some way, either for better or worse. When it comes to choosing friends, you have to choose wisely. You don't want to be living a life full of regrets because of some people who were supposed to help you get through life. If you have too much negativity around you, it can affect the way you think and make wrong decisions . It's best if you surround yourself with people who are positive and who want to invest more in improving their lives. It's important to have people around you because it can make you feel better about yourself. But you also need to watch out for the negative ones who bring the energy level down. They can make you think more negatively about things, not giving you the chance to look at things in a different perspective.

Perhaps it's time that we take a moment and think about who is surrounding us, bringing energy up or dragging it down. It might help if we try to surround ourselves with people whose mindset is more positive rather than dealing with those who attract negativity. Surround yourself with positivity!

Don't compare yourself to others

You are you, not them. Don't try to be like anyone else. You are you. There is only one you. You are special and wonderful in your own way, accept it. If you try to be like someone else you will never know who you really are.

If you don't love yourself you can't love others. If you don't know yourself how do expect to know what true happiness is? There's a difference between loving yourself and narcissism. Narcissists are obsessed with themselves, they don't love themselves the way they are supposed to. They think they are better than everyone else around them. Real self-love is when you can appreciate your own strengths as well as accept your weaknesses even if you feel like you are hiding them from other people.

Self-Love doesn't mean selfishness or that you should love yourself at the cost of others. You should be kind to yourself and treat yourself the way that you would want another person to treat you, but keep in mind that sometimes it's okay to put yourself first, just don't forget where your priorities should lie first before anyone else's because by putting someone else first does not necessarily mean that their needs will be met before your own.

Don't let others put you down. Put yourself out there! You are amazing and no one can tell you otherwise. Question the people who try to bring you down because they are probably unhappy with themselves. Don't compare yourself to anyone else but always be willing to learn from others so that it will help you grow.

People who always compare themselves to others are never happy with themselves. They are always trying to be someone else and they can never be content with who they are. They also tend to be very judgmental of others and they may not even realize it.

Believe in yourself and you will be successful.

Self-confidence is key to success. If you don't believe in yourself, no one else will. Successful people know this and work to cultivate a positive self-image. This allows them to take risks and achieve great things.

Self-confidence comes from being comfortable with who you are. Many people have a negative self-image because they don't know themselves well enough. They may feel that certain aspects of their personality or appearance prevent them from being successful, and therefore they shy away from new challenges.

The solution to this problem is knowledge - the more you know about yourself, the better. If you can look in the mirror and honestly say "I like who I am," then you're on your way to success.

How do we become confident?

Positive thinking will help you become more confident over time. But there's an old saying; "you can't think your way into right actions." Although positive thinking is important, it won't make you confident unless you also take steps to improve your life. One step is knowing yourself better.

Many people are uncomfortable with themselves because they don't understand their own values or motivations enough. They may wish they were more funny, or good at sports, but if these aren't really part of who they are, then it's futile to try and change them. Discovering what you're good at and what makes you happy is important, just as much as learning which aspects of your personality need work.

This process requires introspection - watching yourself closely and thinking about why you act in certain ways. You can do this by keeping a journal or diary, writing down how you feel after certain events every day. This will help build self-awareness and give you a stronger sense of who you really are.

Self-confidence is not something that comes from "being told" that you're good enough. You have to prove to yourself that your goals are achievable because in the end, it's all up to you. If you want success, then just remember this - Believe in yourself and you will be successful.

Positive attitude, don't give up when things get hard!

When times get tough, often you want to give up. Don't do it! When times get tough, it's important to keep a positive attitude and not give up on it. Why not? Because giving up is like saying that you're giving up on yourself, and if you give up on yourself, then who else will? And we don't want anybody to stop believing in themselves.

If you keep a positive attitude, even when times get tough – and they will – you can meet the challenges head-on and come through them without anything holding you back. If somebody tells you that something's impossible or tells you "no", remember: You are capable of so much more than what people tell you. Remember how far you've come before now! Everyone starts out with nothing, but if someone says it's impossible for somebody coming from nothing to have success... Well everyone has to start somewhere! Remember where you've been, and then look to the future. Don't be discouraged by what others think of you. Be proud of who you are!

You may have been told you're not good enough, but what others think doesn't matter. You are a unique individual and nobody in the world can do what you do in the way that you do it. That's why it's so important to love yourself for who you are because if you don't love yourself, then how on Earth are you going to love anybody else?

If you've been told you're not good enough before... Well, who are they to say what's good enough for you? You know yourself better than anyone else. And if someone doesn't see your worth then that just means that it's time for them to move on and for you to surround yourself with people who really do appreciate you for you.

So how can you keep a positive attitude? Well, it's not always easy, but there are a few things you can do. First, make sure to take care of yourself physically. Get enough sleep, eat healthy foods, and exercise regularly. This will help your body feel good and give you the energy to face the day.

Second, make time for things you enjoy. Whether it's reading, writing, painting, listening to music, or spending time with friends and family, do something that makes you happy every day.

And lastly, stay positive in your thoughts. Don't let negative thoughts bring you down – replace them with positive ones! When you start to think "I can't do this" or "I'm not good enough", stop yourself and tell yourself "I can do this" and "I am good enough".

It's important to remember that at the end of the day, you are your own best friend and only cheerleader. Nobody's opinion about yourself matters more than yours does.

Goals setting is an important step to take to achieve anything you want in life

No one can make your dreams come true but you. You are the only person who is responsible for achieving what you want to achieve in life. And it's not just about making a living, either—it's also about finding satisfaction and happiness on this earth. So ask yourself:

What do I really want?

What does my heart tell me?

What goals am I willing to set myself so that I might attain them?

What do I want to know about myself?

No one else can answer these questions. Only you can. And it's important that you do. Write them down somewhere where they won't be easily forgotten or discarded when the going gets tough. The more specific these goals are, the better—it will help keep them from being just vague wishes that have no direction or substance .

Setting goals for yourself is an important part of knowing who you are. No one can make your dreams come true but you, and it's up to you to decide what kind of life you want. Your decisions will affect the course your life takes, so it's a good idea to take some time and think about what matters most in this world.

Once you know what you want to accomplish in your life, you'll be able to make the choices necessary for achieving your goals—the choices, for example, about where you want to go to school; how much time you should devote to your job; whether or not you want to get married and/or have children; the kind of place where you want to live.

The decisions that will affect your life are many and varied. You'll also need courage if you're going to make these choices because they can mean taking a path different from what your friends and family might advocate. But in the end, the success of what you decide will be up to you. And remember: As long as we live we still have our dreams ahead of us.

So we must try again and again until we succeed in achieving our goals no matter how.

So what are you waiting for?

Set some goals today, and then go out there and get them!

Belongingness by Abraham Maslow

According to Abraham Maslow, people need to feel a sense of belongingness in order to be happy and satisfied with their lives. He developed this theory based on his observations of people who were self-actualized. These people were able to find fulfillment and satisfaction in their lives by being part of a community or group. Maslow found that these people also shared similar characteristics, including a strong sense of compassion. He claimed that they were able to have this compassion because they felt connected to others in the community.

Maslow studied self-actualized people who he believed had reached their full potential as human beings. He identified various characteristics that many of these individuals shared, such as creativity and spontaneity. He believed that individuals who feel a sense of belongingness develop these characteristics because they are free from feelings of isolation or alienation. They instead have a strong feeling of community and support, allowing them to explore different aspects of themselves and their interests.

Individuals who lack a sense of belongingness can experience problems such as depression and low self-esteem. These people often turn to dangerous behaviors such as drug use in an attempt to satisfy the need for social connection. Although individuals may try to replace this need by turning to drugs, Maslow found that this is not possible because drugs do not satisfy the need for acceptance and community involvement.

In order for people to be truly happy, they must feel part of something bigger than themselves. So consider these aspects when thinking about the way you want to shape your life.

Section 3: The Importance of Being Proud of Who You Are!

Pride is a characteristic that we should all strive to have. It's what separates successful people from failures. Pride in oneself and pride in one's work will help you feel more satisfied and fulfilled with your life. Pride means accepting yourself for who you are. When you accept your true self, you won't seek others to fill in the gaps or become what they want you to be. The more confident you are with yourself and who you are, the more fascinating of a person that you'll appear to others.

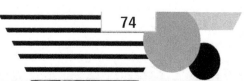

Accepting yourself can be one of the hardest things to do, but it is one of the most important steps towards living a happy life. Pride in oneself and pride in what you do will help you feel more satisfied and fulfilled with your life, which will result in a less stressful lifestyle. This can uplift the moods of everyone around you! So, take some time today and think about your identity. If you're unhappy with an aspect of it, decide and commit to changing it for the better! If there's anything that makes me feel alive and proud of who I am, it's when I find ways to help my fellow man. When I help strangers realize their strengths and be comfortable with who they are, I always feel proud of the person I'm working with.

There is no way to be proud of who you are unless you first love yourself. Once you understand this, everything else will fall into place. If you are proud of who you are, nothing will stand in your way from achieving your goals.

Why is it important to be proud of who you are?

The answer is simple. It is important because it builds self-esteem! Self-esteem is the measure of your opinion of yourself. When you feel good about yourself, your success rate increases dramatically. This can be seen in business, sports, and education. As humans we are impacted by the thoughts we think and act out! Self-esteem leads to positive thoughts; which, in turn, leads to better decisions, which leads to better performance, which leads to higher self-esteem! Ultimately, this means a more proud you! Here are a few actions that you can take towards self-love and self-worth:

1) Acknowledge your own value even if others don't
2) Respect yourself enough to put yourself first
3) Take care of your mental and physical health
4) Start doing things for yourself!
5) Get a night of good sleep.
6) Exercise.
7) Practice positive self-talk.
8) Use the power of your mind. It is important to be proud of who you are because it is through your mind that you will be transformed. Every time you think about yourself, you build a positive image in your mind.
9) More positive thoughts. The more positive thoughts you have, the more people will like you. In short, your mind is your best friend!
10) Be grateful and thankful. Proud of who you are means you should be incredibly grateful for the opportunities you have.
11) Be confident because you are confident. When you believe in yourself and your ability, you have the power to change your life. When you are confident, everything you do becomes easier.

Anything is possible with a little more confidence! Never doubt yourself. Never let anyone else tell you what you can't do!

12) Be open to new opportunities. Become comfortable with who you are and take a chance to change your life! Do not be afraid to be proud of who you are because it will lead to new opportunities for you!

13) Be curious. Ask questions and get to know yourself! A little self-knowledge means a lot to you!

14) Be optimistic & Envision the best. You are better than you think, so be proud of who you are!

15) Be grateful for what you have as this will help you will have more in the future!

16) Be friendly & kind to others. Being proud and confident is a great way to show love and kindness to others. These qualities are contagious. Be humble and grateful to others and they will be grateful to you.

17) Stay true to yourself. You are the only person who knows what's right for you. You are the only person who knows what makes you happy. Be proud of who you are because you are special and you are unique!

18) Be happy. You are the only one who can control your happiness.

How to Confidently Confront Others With Your Ideas & Beliefs?

Everyone wants to be heard, but it can be difficult to confidently confront others with your ideas and beliefs when they disagree or oppose you. With some consideration and preparation, you'll be able to confidently voice your opinions and make a lasting impact on the world. Here are some tips to help you become a confident person and make your ideas heard:

1) Know your beliefs

2) Have a plan.

3) Be firm but soft-spoken.

4) Don't take it personally.

5) Forgive.

Section 4: What is a Growth Mindset

In 2013, Psychologist Angela Lee Duckworth introduced a short but motivational speech in TED Talk. She asked, "...what if doing well in life depends on much more than your ability to learn quickly and easily?" And her answer to this question was relatively new, if not revolutionary.

Through years of research, Duckworth and her team identified the most significant predictor of success—and it's not social skills, appearance, physical health, and even IQ; instead, it was grit. Duckworth explained grit as "passion and perseverance for very long-term goals." Grit is building the stamina to stick to your perceived goals for years and working hard to achieve them. In different educational and work settings, grit accurately predicted the success of the persons therein. This brings us to this relevant question: what does grit have to do with a growth mindset?

By definition, a growth mindset is a belief that an individual can develop skills, talents, abilities, and intelligence by exerting effort. Like grit, the growth mindset is the persistence to succeed by embracing challenges, accepting criticisms constructively, and powering through setbacks. Comparatively, people with a fixed mindset believe that their talents and intelligence are: innate, handed down by nature as it is, and/or something that cannot be changed.

To further differentiate, this is how people with a fixed mindset think:

> "I just can't learn math."
> "I simply have no talent for singing."
> "I can't swim because of my height."
> "I didn't get the job because I'm not fit for it."

When people think this way, they are programmed to believe they are incapable because that's how they are and always will be, believing it's an inborn trait. But what do people with a growth mindset think? They think like this:

> "If I keep studying, I'll be better at math."
> "If I take vocal lessons seriously, I can sing well."
> "If I attend swimming classes, I'll learn how to swim."
> "I should improve my skills to get the job."

Unlike people with a fixed mindset, persons with a growth mindset understand that their talents and intelligence can improve with effort, motivation, and engagement. In a classroom setting or at an educational level, these two varying mindsets manifest in school grades, test scores, and passing rates. A growth mindset fosters lower failure rates, improved scores, increased effort, more problems solved, and a higher level of achievement. But the same also applies to life in general.

The thing about fixed mindset is it sets the precedent that what you can't do is something you can't do with permanence when, in fact, it just requires grit to be able to do it. Instead of saying, "I can't do it," say, "I'm still learning, and I'll keep trying." With this, you rewire your brain to see the possibilities of putting in the effort. Your internal dialogue translates into your external actions. Here are more examples of how you shouldn't and should talk to yourself:

From: "I suck at this." **To:** "How can I be better at this?"
From: "I'm not good enough." **To:** "I can still do more."
From: "This is too hard." **To:** "I should practice. It will get easier."
From: "I might make a mistake." **To:** "It's okay to make mistakes—it's a lesson!"
From: "I'm not as good as the others." **To:** "I should learn from them."
From: "I don't know how." **To:** "I can learn how!"
From: "I give up." **To:** "I'll keep trying!"

The key to success lies in the effort you put into everything you do. Effort begins from having the will to do it—it's in your mind. As Albert Einstein said: "Genius is 1% talent and 99% hard work." And hard work is developing a growth mindset and employing grit. After all, even geniuses work hard.

Section 5: How To Develop A Growth Mindset

How you see yourself and how you perceive the world is what is known as your mindset. Since everyone is unique, we don't always see everything eye-to-eye. The debate of the half-full, half-empty glass resurfaces again. Likewise, two particular mindsets rose to popularity as the primary approach of persons in terms of life's successes and challenges. This is the growth and fixed mindset—you either think you worked hard enough to be called gifted or you're just naturally gifted, as introduced in the previous chapter.

Admittedly, being naturally gifted sounds like the better option. But thinking it is what it is or "I was just born this way" is a fixed mindset that makes you avoid problems, give up easily, not put in the effort, ignore criticism, and feel threatened by the success of others. Would you rather be someone who doesn't believe in practice and hard work? Or would you instead develop and improve your talents, skills, abilities, and intelligence to learn and succeed? If you chose the latter, you made the right choice. So, now, you have to learn how to foster a growth mindset.

Before doing so, first, we must understand that a growth mindset isn't just about working harder and smarter; it's about your attitude toward failure and achievement. When you're faced with a setback, you're supposed to get back up and try again. Likewise, when you're rewarded with a feat, you should strive for more significant success. To attain this mindset, here are four simple tips:

1. *Start Small*

To know where to begin, you must identify which mindset you have been employing to this day. Have you been unconsciously practicing a growth mindset or a fixed mindset? Did you strive for what you have achieved so far, or was it just handed to you? Knowing where you are is the primary step to knowing where to go next.

Now, ask yourself why you want a growth mindset—and don't just answer with the general conclusion of motivation, benefits, and success. Instead, think about how it will make your life better. Will it make you more confident? Will it give you a sense of satisfaction? If finding the answer to this seems complicated on your own, seek other people—people who have already incorporated this into their lives. Gain insights from their experience. Or maybe you could find someone who also wants to develop the same mindset, and perhaps you can take this journey with them.

If the human experience doesn't satisfy your curiosity, turn to science. Learn about neuroplasticity, or the brain's ability to rewire itself. Understanding how you can "train" your brain to master the growth mindset may bring you more clarity about its relevance.

The bottom line is mastery is a step-by-step process. So, take your time and enjoy the journey.

2. *Understand Success and Failure*

Success and failure is a pre-requisite of life. At any point in our lives, we either meet setbacks or get rewarded for our hard work. No matter how far we come, we'll inevitably face this twin element that could determine or test our capabilities. Since success is something we automatically accept, what we need to change our perspectives on is failures. So often, we see failure as a sign or lack of inability when, in fact, it is an opportunity to learn. Each life challenge is an opportunity to grow, improve and do better. It is more than a problem that needs to be solved; it is learning and growing. Therefore, we should see them in a positive light.

To fully appreciate the lessons incorporated in every obstacle in life, spend a moment each day reflecting on the things you failed at and the things you learned from them. Then, instead of beating yourself up, make it a habit to find the silver linings in failure. Appreciate them. Congratulate yourself for getting through them.

Simultaneously, you can also use this moment to write down your achievements, no matter how small. Maybe you took the stairs to your apartment instead of taking the elevator. Perhaps you finished the day without smoking to relieve your stress. You cleaned your room. You drank eight glasses of water today. Celebrate every small achievement, for they matter to your overall success. This can even be a way to motivate yourself to take action toward your ultimate goal. On this note, also celebrate the season of other people. More than celebrating with them, ask them what they did to achieve such success. Their stories can be your reference.

3. *Take it Easy on Yourself*

Before we delve further into this topic, remind yourself that changing your mindset takes time and determination. Thus, there is no need to pressure yourself. In all our goals in our life, they must be realistic. Why? Because trying to achieve something that is beyond what you can do will only burn you out and disappoint you. Humans have certain limitations. Blame genetic makeup or physical health, but some things require more effort. It's like climbing the Himalayas with a weak lung.

But this is not to discourage you from things you have yet to do; this is to help you realize that your success is also based on the things you can do and the things you're good at. Still, if there is something you want to do but wouldn't, it's the perfect time to pay attention to how you speak and act to yourself. Does your inner dialogue say, "I can't do this," or does it say, "I can do this with practice?" Listen to how you speak to yourself because your inner voice will affect your overt actions. So, be kind to yourself. Convince yourself you are capable and act upon these thoughts. A simple technique is to add the word "yet." For example, instead of "I can't do this," say "I can't do this yet." Manifest that the time will come you'll be able to do it.

Finally, when it comes to taking it easy on yourself, you must stop judging yourself. The whole world is already taking part in putting you down, so why be a part of it? Even at times of failure, don't ever look at yourself as unskilled or talentless. You are always more than the things you achieve or fail at. In a world where people laugh when you fall, be the person who pulls yourself up.

4. Change Your Outlook on Life

If life hasn't welcomed you so kindly, continue looking at it with kind eyes. One of the reasons we see the world negatively is that we tend to develop problematic thinking patterns, like seeking approval from the people around us. Continuously seeking approval entails that one would also ignore his own needs and comfort. Hence, the goals you pursue are also likely to be a goal of someone else—for you. So, change your outlook by cultivating self-acceptance.

With a growth mindset, it is equally important to reward actions and not just traits. Shallow compliments mean less compared to praising a person's effort. If being beautiful or intelligent is inherent, praise the way they carry themselves or the effort they put into learning more. Instead of simply looking at the world with fresh eyes, pass it on. Allow others to indulge in the beauty of learning, growing, and succeeding.

Ultimately, the only thing stopping us from achieving our full potential is ourselves. By changing our mindset—and choosing a healthy one, we open ourselves to the endless possibility of continuous progress. Sure, innate intelligence and talents may sound like the better alternative, but a growth mindset improves your quality of life. Don't settle for just who you are; always strive to be more because self-acceptance and success require it.

Section 6: Develop Empowering Routines

Why are people fascinated with success? Is it because success entails fame, comfort, and social status? Or is it because success is interchangeable with happiness? Perhaps, it's purely human nature, where we live our lives long enough to wonder what our ultimate goal is and how we achieve it. While on this topic, surely, we all wondered what's the secret to success. Call it luck, wealth, education, hard work, or connections, but the one ultimate thing successful people share is this: they stick to a particular routine.

A routine is a group of activities you engage with repeatedly and religiously. It's a set of tasks you vow to accomplish daily, weekly, or monthly. So, why is it relevant to success? Because routines establish great habits and, in turn, bring you closer to your goals. But the idea of routine does not refer to just any routine; this refers to empowering routines.

Empowering routines continuously allow you to stick to particular activities that help you advance toward your goal. For it to be continuous, it must be undemanding—you must be able to do it even without forging daily plans and schedules. If you have to consciously decide on your plans, it's a disempowering routine—hence, demanding and exhausting to commit to every day and more likely to fail. It also pertains to tasks that keep you busy and not productive. Like entertaining boredom with random internet browsing, working in a job you don't like, worrying about your situation but not taking action to improve it, or wasting your time on pointless, toxic, and abusive relationships. These are only a few examples.

As you will learn, incorporating bad routines will only trap you in a cycle of dissatisfaction and unhappiness. The next thing you know, you are living a life that doesn't feed your soul. But how will you know if you're already on the path of soulless living? Here are some warning signs:

1. You always feel bored, uninspired, or unfulfilled with your life.
2. Your daily activities feel like chores or work to you.
3. You wish you could do something else with your life but feel like you don't have a choice.
4. You feel busy, but you don't see your progress.
5. You feel constantly tired even when you don't do much.

If these signs apply to you, it's time to develop empowering routines.

The importance of establishing routines lies in the fact that already-developed habits are easier to maintain. It becomes secondary to your nature—ingrained in your body and mind that you do it on autopilot. As a beginner, you can start with making your bed, staying hydrated, exercising, going for walks, and watering your plants. Do any of which—or whatever you wish to do—daily until it becomes a habit. Once you achieve this, progress to more significant routines like meditating, writing in your journal, allotting time strictly for work and leisure, ticking off things on your bucket list, and tracking your progress and productivity. These are keys to transcending into high-level routines like figuring out your life's vision, long-term goals, and personal ethics.

To live your best life, you are required to cross the bridge between vision and reality. Powerful routines allow you to do this. By aligning your routine to your goals, your visions become achievements, all because you are progressively acting on your plans.

One thing you must ensure about empowering routines is that your chosen day-to-day activities must energize you. Apart from aligning them with your goals, they must connect with your morals and values. Good energy reverberates to the people around you. And frankly, nothing is more empowering than being surrounded by people encouraging you to do and feel better.

As always, be mindful; not all empowering routines work for you. Allow yourself to try, and even fail, at some until you can find the best ones that work for you. Remove activities that drain you. Add activities that energize you. Upgrade your routine so it fulfills you.

Whatever you choose to do, no matter how monotonous it may seem, understand that repetition is a routine, and routine is a habit. Habits make you productive, creative, and mentally fit. Ultimately, there is power in personal automation—it cultivates the many wonders of the mind. So, this is your sign of giving it a try.

Section 7: Change And Improve Your Self Image

So, you're insecure. You hate the freckles on your face and the height of your hairline. You wish you looked like one of the popular girls. Maybe you dread attending gym class because you aren't as tall or built as the other boys. You wonder why they get more attention than you do without even trying. As you grow older, you wonder why your peers are more successful than you; you check which ones bought a new car or a new house or which ones got a promotion. Who's running their own business? Who's enjoying their fulfilled lives? And whenever you look at your reflection in the mirror, you only feel dissatisfied. When you think about yourself, you only get anxious. When you look at your achievements, you feel lacking. You don't like what you see, you hate how you feel, and you're dissatisfied with who you are right now. You find yourself asking: why am I like this? Why am I too fat? Why am I so unhappy? All these questions are directed at your self-image.

Self-image is the mental picture you have of yourself—physical image, individuality, personality, body image, and gender. It defines, if not dictates, what you can and cannot achieve in life. It is a collection of how you see yourself, how you wish to see yourself, and how others see you. It is the manifestation of ourselves from the human psyche and society simultaneously. Unbeknownst to some, self-image can actually determine successful relationships—or success in general—and satisfy the sense of well-being. But on the other hand, it can cause self-defeating and self-destructive behaviors. Thus, improving your self-image matters. How? By reconnecting with yourself.

To reconnect with yourself, there are five questions you must ask. Ask yourself the following, one after another:

1. Who am I?

Poor self-image makes you lose sight of who you are; that old cheerful, happy-go-lucky girl is now lonely and anxious about everything. In answering this question, write your thoughts down. Answer who am I right now? Write down your qualities, values, and beliefs—negative and positive. Consider each answer and recognize them as a part of you. Which ones do you want to bring along in your life's journey? Which ones should you leave behind as it impedes your growth? Write them down and evaluate them.

2. Why do I have to change?

Now that you've written down your negative beliefs or traits that could be your downfall, you must understand why change is essential. The thing is, some of your personal views have been holding you back from your personal growth. It may be easier to sweep them under the rug, but by doing so, you allow the same unnecessary thoughts to weigh you down. Knowing they exist, recognizing them, and deciding not to let them hinder you is a step in the right direction. Change is only scary if it serves you no advantage--this one does.

3. Where can I draw inspiration from?

It's simply torturing to do something that doesn't make you happy. How can you change or improve your self-image if it feels like a chore to do so? Thus, find something that will inspire you to achieve this. Perhaps, find a person whose confidence you adore. Admire him or her and pick up the qualities you want to incorporate into your life. And no, you're not supposed to compare yourself with this person—that's destructive behavior. Instead, you are using them as an example. After all, there's a reason you adore this person. Perhaps, you can adore yourself with it too.

4. Who do I want to be?

If the question "why do I have to change" focuses on your negative traits, this time, you focus on your positive qualities. Redefine yourself around your good qualities. Instead of just pointing them out, turn them into better traits. Expand it. Improve it. Embrace it. You can also incorporate the characteristics you wish you have. From there, slowly commit yourself to become the person you envisioned. Surely, that person is happier and more content than you are. So, aim to be that person.

5. *Do I feel good about it?*

So, you've started to refine your self-image. You figured out which thinking patterns have been bringing you down and which ones you could work on—and that's great. Now, close your eyes and visualize yourself being the person you aspire to be. Could you really be that person? Does that person feel right? If yes, start "rehearsing" the new you. Slowly allow your vision to leak into your reality.

Before we discuss the many feasible steps for improving self-image, we must also realize that self-image is affected by our potential—or at least by the things we believe we are capable of. Limitations on our performance are both real and imagined, some of which are self-imposed. Likewise, if you are caged by thoughts that there are only limited things you can and could do, your mindset would look like this:

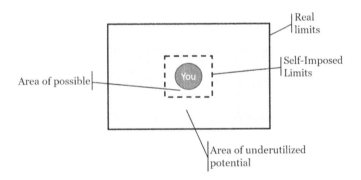

As you can see, the area of possible is minimal compared to your under-utilized potential. It's kept minimal because of self-imposed limitations. In reality, the only thing that should be keeping you from utilizing your full potential is real limitations; it could be physical incapability or sheer impossibility. But it should never be your mindset—not your fears, worries, anxieties, and a false sense of security. Once you achieve a stable and improved self-image, your mindset will only have a wide area of possibility, manageable self-imposed limitations, and real limitations. There should be no room for under-utilized potential because keeping such would mean you've set poor goals for yourself solely based on self-doubting beliefs. Here is an illustration:

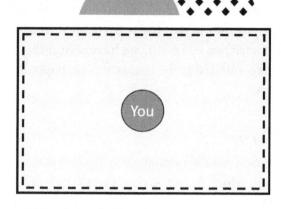

The secret to unlearning self-doubting beliefs lies in improving your self-image. Answering questions and recognizing potentials and limitations become superficial knowledge if one does not exert the effort to actually improve. Thus, here are some examples of how to improve your self-image:

1. Understand the science behind self-image

In the study of cybernetics, the brain and the nervous system create a "goal-striving mechanism." Depending on how you operate towards it, such mechanism can be satisfied with success or compromised with failure. Since humans are driven by achievements and goals, there is always something we strive for. In terms of self-image, our brain sets a goal that is borne from our thinking patterns. For example, if we fill our heads with thoughts of worry, guilt, fears, or failures, our subconscious mind receives negative imagery that reduces our goals. In effect, our motivation, attitude, and body language adapt similarly.

The science behind self-image states that how you view yourself affects your motivations—thus, it could motivate or limit you.

2. Act on the change you perceive

If you imagine yourself as fit and healthy, don't leave it as imagination. Act on it. This means if you smoke, quit smoking. If you drink a lot, reduce drinking. If you binge eat, avoid it. If you don't exercise, start now. The thing about acting on the change you want is that you must have both the mindset and the lifestyle of your perception.

For example, in smoking. If you want to become a non-smoker, you should act like a non-smoker. Apart from acting on it, you must also condition your brain into thinking that you are not a smoker. Instead of saying, "I haven't smoked in a week," say, "I am a non-smoker for a week now." Incorporate a sense of achievement with how you view yourself as you transform into a new and improved version of yourself.

Understand that your creative mental picture can turn into a positive goal mechanism that subconsciously changes your behavior and attitude.

3. Appreciate and compliment yourself

People with positive self-image begin the chain of positivity within themselves. So, it should start with you too. Appreciate yourself through compliments; tell yourself you're attractive, intelligent, or talented. Spoil yourself with words of affirmation—because you don't need it from anybody else. So, if you feel underdressed, take a few more minutes to wear something that makes you look at yourself with a smile.

A positive self-image starts within you. Always. There is nothing more important than how you see yourself. When you achieve a sense of satisfaction for who you are, how other people see you become irrelevant.

4. Engage in non-judgmental reflection

To work on your self-critical and unhealthy thinking patterns, you must identify which mental habits are disruptive to your growth. So, reflect on yourself, not so you can criticize yourself, but so you can acknowledge them and improve on them.

Another mode of reflection is relaxation. Once you've supplied your goal to your subconscious, let willpower give you the answers to how you should achieve them. Sometimes, in matters of the mind, putting in an effort will only mess with your natural progress—some ideas are meant to come to you as it is. So, don't force it.

5. Be Inspired by Role Models

There's a thin line between jealousy and inspiration. And when seeking answers to fill your soul, always choose the latter.

Frankly, the world is filled with people to look up to, so finding people to inspire you to embrace a positive self-image is not hard work. First, find them so you can learn from them; see how they behave, how they talk about their lives, which great qualities do they possess, and what makes them confident? When you identify these things, add them to your own repertoire. Then, instead of comparing yourself to them, fill the gap between your differences and embrace the change it comes with. Thinking you cannot be like them is a self-imposed limitation that hinders you from exploring all your possibilities. So, choose a positive role model and follow in their footsteps.

6. *Develop a winner's image*

A winner's image is a byproduct of a positive self-image. As the name suggests, a winner's image will make you think, feel, act, and be a winner. Achieving this takes patience and commitment, where three phases must be completed: fantasy, theory, and fact.

In fantasy, you have to realize that most inventions began as fantasies inside someone's head, like how Thomas Edison imagined the lightbulb and later built it. Here, the only requirement for you is to choose your fantasy. Then, under theory, you must shift your attitude according to your fantasy. Ask yourself, "how will I accomplish this?" Finally, the fact phase. Here your fantasy can evolve into a fact—whatever you're fantasies are, make it real. To do that, you have to have the skills and the devotion.

Knowing that self-image is correlated to self-confidence, you have to work on the latter to allow yourself to smoothly translate this confidence to the world—an ingredient to success. Appreciating who you are, identifying your lack, and actively working on yourself will change your life. What matters in life is not how other people see you; it's about seeing yourself as the person you always perceived to be—happy and successful. Maybe even more. Labels are not the only factor that differentiates successful people from the rest—they choose to separate themselves and work on it.

Truthfully, there is no one secret sauce to a positive self-image, but expanding how you view yourself is a surefire way to establish it. The thing about envisioning yourself as someone better and more capable is that it subconsciously lets you find ways to live by your new and improved version. Who you are today is not someone lacking—who you are today is someone that can do better. That better person in your head can be you if you just put in the effort. So, breathe as calmly as that person would. Stand the same way that person would stand. Walk like him, talk like him, gesture like him, live like him—with the same passion and consistency. With consistency, your brain will develop it as a habit, and habits form part of who you are. Belief becomes a mindset. The mindset becomes behavior. Behavior becomes you—naturally. So, expand how you see yourself. Imagine the person you want to be and become that person.

Section 8: Effective Ways To Improve Your Confidence

Since a positive self-image is related to confidence, the most obvious way to improve your self-image is to improve your confidence. For the sake of being honest, let's all admit that we all want to be confident. Because why not?

Confident people shine the brightest in one room—always with their heads held high, seemingly without an ounce of worry about themselves. They see themselves positively. But confident people aren't always just born; some are also made. And if you have yet to become confident, we can make you one. But first, remember that self-image is developed from how you see yourself, how you want to see yourself, and how others see you. Hence, you need to work on your confidence on a personal, mental, and social level.

Personal Level

Growth takes time, and change is overwhelming, so it is essential to understand that improving your confidence doesn't have to feel like working with a deadline. Instead, feel free to start small and slow. Instead of pressuring yourself into a change you might not be too comfortable with, make small, realistic promises to yourself—nothing grand or hard to commit to.

You can make small personal promises by smiling to make you seem calm and collected in a given but appropriate situation. Exercising as it triggers happy hormones, reduces stress, and makes you feel amazing. Grooming because showering and putting on perfume is not just vain but builds self-esteem. Dressing nicely to make you feel good about yourself—appear attractive and presentable. Doing activities you enjoy to soothe yourself and help you identify your talents and skills. Finally, sitting up straight and walking tall lift your mood. Sounds simple, right? Simple and doable.

Mental Level

While the physical level is easier to commit to, preparing yourself for the mental battle of gaining self-confidence requires more patience and even more determination, but hard work pays off. To start, you first have to identify the root problem of your low self-confidence. Is it because you afraid of failing or rejection? If so, remember that failure and rejection are part of the growth process, and everyone goes through it. Is it because your anxiety gives you the harshest assumptions and feedback? Then, rewrite the narrative in your head. Talk back and say otherwise if your mind tells you you're not good enough. Do it each time it speaks ill about you. Do it until it comes to you naturally. Be the cheerleader you need; only say words of kindness and affirmation to yourself. Or are your emotions and feelings holding you back? If so, you must remember that positive or negative emotions come to an end. It's temporary, and it's what makes you human.

But whatever it is that's stopping you from being confident, focus on your intention. Why do you want to be confident? There is no wrong or correct answer, but rest assured that confidence will bring you a sense of satisfaction. So, adopt a growth mindset, focus on what you can control, face uncomfortable situations without running away, and accept yourself for who you are.

Social Level

So, you've given yourself more attention and made peace with your mind. What's next? Work on the people around you. The fact of the matter is this: no one really cares about you that much—the world does not revolve around you. So, all this excessive worrying about what you're doing, how you look, and who you are is not that big of a deal. There's no need to please anyone or attain perfection. Everybody else is preoccupied enough with their own lives. People caring about you that much is but an illusion, a figment of your fears.

But why the hard truth? Because you only have to work on yourself for yourself—not for anybody else. If you need to please the people around you, maybe it's time to find a like-minded community that cultivates a shared experience of the journey toward self-confidence. On this note, maybe you should also step away from social media. Studies show that social media promotes a "false self" that gives you a false sense of self-worth.

Instead of virtual relationships, reconnect with the people around you. Sympathize with yourself and the people you're surrounded with, or focus on someone you want to learn from.

Self-confidence and self-image come hand-in-hand in life. At the end of the day, achieving our life's aspirations depend on how much we believe we can do something. Confidence is an excellent fuel to keep going in life, this time with a better perspective of yourself.

Section 9: The Benefits Of Thinking Big

In matters of success, everyone starts small. As a toddler, you first learn how to crawl before you can walk. In school, you learn your ABCs before your subject-verb agreement. In work, your superiors train you before assigning you to a project with minimal supervision. In life, you have to try and fail before ultimately getting things right. Hence, you start small—always. But in a world where everyone agrees that starting small is key to everything, what happens when starting small is partnered with thinking big?

To think big means to condition your mind to imagine and visualize all positive possibilities in your life. It's conceiving great thoughts where you make smarter decisions and act on them to achieve goals. "Think big, aim high, act bold." Gary Keller added, "And see just how big you can blow up your life." Hence, we venture to the benefits of thinking big—because they're bigger than you can imagine. Here are some of the things big thinkers acquire:

Motivation and Drive

When you think big, you spark your motivation and drive to act on your goals; but it's not just any goal—it's a goal that excites you. But, unfortunately, one of the reasons why some people are unmotivated with what they're doing in their life is because it doesn't excite them. It doesn't make their blood pump, and it doesn't make them want to get up every morning to get things done. However, big thinkers' goals come from a place of passion, making goals a work of choice and a voluntary chore.

Connections and Opportunities

There's a reason why the quote "you attract what you are" is famous. It's because it's true. In reality, your friends are your friends because you share certain similarities with them. Similarly, if you think big, you also attract people with the same mindset. And big thinkers are often successful people—passionate and enthusiastic about their passions. When you attract these people, you open yourself to the right connections and opportunities to learn and grow. With the right peers, the right opportunities come along.

Growth

In therapy, you will learn that immature thinking patterns are some of the many things that hinder your growth. For example, discouraging yourself, blaming others for your failure, or not putting in enough effort stumps your personal growth. But by thinking big, you focus your attention on things that matter: your success. This means you're not afraid to try new things, take responsibility for your mistakes, learn from them, and work hard to get the best results. With this, it isn't just self-esteem that you muster; it's also overall potential for optimal success.

Full Potential

For big thinkers, the world is a place full of nothing but opportunities. Unlike people who limit themselves, big thinkers don't stay inside their comfort zones and settle for what is handed to them—they do everything they can to be successful. They don't let their fears cripple them; if anything, they use them as fuel to keep going. The thing is, you must allow your dreams to scare you a little. That's how you know you're thinking big. Remember, you are the only thing stopping you from becoming everything you aspire to be. If it's not genetic makeup or impossibility, you are limitless. Realistically, you already are.

Given the many benefits of thinking big, how do you think big? Here are some examples:

1. *Imagine great possibilities:* If you see yourself as someone who will become unsuccessful, you will not find the motivation to succeed. So, begin the process by thinking of all the great possibilities you can and will likely achieve.
2. *Read more:* Reading is proven to effectively expand a person's perspective. It is also one of the simplest ways to stimulate thinking, being one of the primary sources of knowledge. So, if your fears disable you from doing something new, ease your mind by reading about it. Sometimes, the answers to our questions are right before us. You just have to read them.
3. *Communicate with like-minded people:* Since thinking big attracts people who also think big, take the opportunity to engage with people who could share similar experiences with you. Instead of feeling bad for not being as great as someone in your circle, reach out and learn from them. It's amazing how other people's success can inspire you.
4. *Think big—as in 10x bigger:* While others groomed themselves to play it safe in life, create big dreams for yourself. Don't settle to become a manager; aspire to be the owner. As long as your dreams are realistic for you, you'll achieve them.
5. *Don't limit yourself:* Roadblocks in life are of natural occurrence, but they are temporary. If you fail a class, it doesn't mean you won't graduate. If you don't have savings right now, it doesn't mean you never will. If you got fired from work, it doesn't mean you won't get one soon. You are the only thing limiting yourself from doing greater things, so stop making the world smaller for yourself.
6. *Plan ahead:* One trait that small thinkers have is that they think short term. For big thinkers, thinking long-term will help you set realistic timelines for your success. Although the future is uncertain, your success can be.
7. *Get curious:* Big thinkers are also curious people. When you're curious, you dream, explore, and discover some more—all the information you gain makes you realize your capabilities and aspirations. You can never know if you're good at writing if you haven't taken the time to sit down and try writing. Keep your curiosity on high to keep your motivation growing.

So, the lesson in thinking big is simple. Take this lesson to you everywhere you go, no matter what you're doing: you achieve what you manifest. When you spend time thinking and imagining what you can achieve, you find yourself subconsciously doing acts that lead you closer to achieving your desired success. As a result, you can become passionate, meet the right people, grow as a person, and live your life the way you're supposed to—to the fullest.

Section 10: Problems = Opportunities

For some people, problems are considered hindrances to success. If you were asked right now, how do you deal with your problems? What would be your answer? If your answer is to sulk in a corner or cry about your problems, then you're one who fails to see that problems are opportunities.

The thing about successful people is that they handle problems with a positive outlook. In their eyes, problems are opportunities to learn, improve, and grow as better people. Of course, successful people still get knocked down on their knees every now and then. Still, their success is associated with their continuous belief that mistakes are opportunities to make things right, problems are opportunities to come up with solutions, and failures are opportunities to try again.

With such a perspective, you are groomed to take advantage of crises—because heroes rise above them in times of crisis. So, why not be the hero in your own crisis? You can, and this is how:

1. *Realize that problems are part of life*

Understandably, we tend to react negatively to problems. You scratched your car at the parking lot, you left your grocery list at home, or your computer shut off before you can turn in your weekly report—unfortunate events happen, and, most of the time, there's nothing we could've done about it. Except for one thing: accept that problems are regular occurrences. When you see problems as something ordinary, it fails to intimidate you and catch you off-guard. It loses its power over-stressing you out and ruining your day. With acceptance, you introduce yourself to a more graceful manner of handling things. You become objective and rational. Soon, you'll become an effective problem-solver.

2. *First impression lasts*

When it comes to first impressions, it doesn't only apply to meeting new people—it also applies to reacting to problems. The thing is, first impressions or reactions to problems define how you would handle the situation. If you find yourself in a middle of a misunderstanding, getting angry would make it harder to fix the problem. So, you have to understand that when it comes to problems, don't make first impressions. Allow yourself to face the problem with ease and rationality. While in an argument, instead of impulsively thinking, "I should just walk out and slam the door behind me," pause. Pause and think of a better plan: "I should listen to his side first before saying anything." Or: "I should ask him to calm down before continuing this conversation."

3. Evaluate problems objectively

Once you get past the emotional stage, dealing with problems becomes easier. After all, a clear mind is a great partner in making sound decisions. To think objectively, you can try describing the situation as if it happened to somebody else. For example, ask yourself, "If my friend told me she was in an argument with her partner about this problem, what advice would I give her?" With this, you get to weigh which solutions are realistic for the situation. Is the problem real or imaginary? Can it be resolved at the moment, or do you need time to think it through? Asking these questions stops you from self-destructive, last-minute thoughts.

4. Focus more on the solution

Allowing a problem to take up too much room in your mind only increases your anxiety and overthinking. So, instead of the problem, focus on the solution. Since the problem is already there, the best thing you can do is solve it. So, how will you proceed now that the argument has happened and the ball is in your court? Let's say you decided to wait until your partner has calmed down. Now what? Consider your options for solving the problem. You can talk to him again. You can apologize. You can comfort him with acts of love. Focus on what happens after the problem. Not on the problem itself.

The takeaway in this subject is this: problems are variables we can't control. From personal dilemmas to purely bad luck, we always have the option to see the problem as an opportunity to learn acceptance, control emotions, choose rationality over emotions, and test problem-solving skills. When we see problems as opportunities to grow as persons, we discover that unfortunate events are life lessons in disguise.

Section 11: The Benefits Of Practicing Gratitude

The attitude of gratitude is not only an appealing catchphrase but also a way of life. But what is it? The attitude of gratitude pertains to consciously and habitually appreciating things in life. As the name itself dictates, it's practicing gratitude for your relationships, health, career, and overall sense of well-being. But other than appreciating the things around you, extend your appreciation for the people and things around you. So, how does gratitude improve your life and increase your odds of success in life? By shifting your mindset.

Practicing gratitude fills you with positivity and purpose. And doing it every day allows you to develop a healthy habit that makes you focus on good things, feel confident, optimistic, and joyful, and replace overwhelming thoughts with feelings of abundance. So, here are three easy ways to develop an attitude of gratitude:

1. *Be grateful daily*

Since an attitude of gratitude is a habit, practicing the same should be done on a daily basis. So, practice gratitude daily and actively. Practice active gratitude—this means consciously finding things to be grateful for and expressing your appreciation. Unlike reactive gratitude, don't wait for something good to happen to show your appreciation. For example, instead of saying thanks because you received flowers today, thank the postman who delivers your post each morning because why not?

2. *Surround yourself with grateful people*

In all your personal ventures, finding people who nurture the same virtue as you is essential. Remember, the people around you can affect your mindset. So, find someone who has a mindset of gratitude. In doing so, you multiply your appreciation—you'll be happier, more optimistic, and more motivated. A positive environment is a great place to grow gratitude.

3. *Commit yourself to gratefulness*

The attitude of gratitude is a habit. Hence, committing to it daily is the best way to incorporate such beautiful change. When you commit to something, you master it, and it soon comes to you naturally. The more important thing with this mindset is that the positive effect ripples from you and the people around you. Gratitude is infectious when done genuinely.

If you still have reservations about practicing gratitude, you must be introduced to the scientifically proven benefits of gratefulness. As already established, grateful people have better relationships, improved physical and psychological health, enhanced empathy, reduced aggression, and higher self-esteem.

These benefits shouldn't come to anyone as a surprise since gratitude is such a refreshing trait. For example, saying thank you to a co-worker who waited for you by the elevator can turn him into a friend. Appreciation also makes people more inclined to maintain their current status, such as good health. They are also inclined to act appropriately in social settings, where they're more likely to behave correctly and cause less trouble. With gratitude, grateful people find themselves less vulnerable to comparing themselves to others, thus, making them more secure and confident.

The good thing about an attitude of gratitude is that it's easy to cultivate. With the right amount of motivation and effort, you can emerge back into the harsh world with kind eyes and an even kinder mouth.

| Part 4 | Make it Happen

Section 1: The Importance of Setting Your Goals and Develop a Plan

It is an undisputed reality that goals are a primary factor in achieving professional and personal success. As early as primary school, we were already asked what we aspired to be when we were older. In secondary school, we considered what courses to take after high school and then, later on, filled out college application forms based on what we wanted to do. In college, we enroll in the degree we wish to pursue. Right after, we find a job based on our education, skills, or experience. Throughout the many phases of life, goals have been steering us toward fulfilling them.

But why is having goals relevant? What's the advantage of sticking to a goal? Why is it so essential to create a plan for achieving goals? In this chapter, we answer all that.

First, goals allow our brains to set up the right mindset and mental conditions to motivate us to achieve the particular goal we've made. Scientists, psychologists, and neurologists have all agreed that goals prepare and push the brain into investing and accomplishing things that it knows are important to us. Similarly, in every hobby, we prepare to start it. For example, if we want to paint, we first buy paintbrushes, paints, and canvasses. We may even assign a room in the house to be our painting studio. Then, we begin visualizing the art and painting it from one stroke to the next. This is what the brain does when we create a goal: it mentally prepares us for it, helps us start, and motivates us to keep going. After all, goals are long-term plans—just one step from our overall vision in life.

Having goals is relevant because it makes people strive harder by setting up plans and working on them continuously. Studies reveal that ambitious people have better performance and satisfactory outputs than those who aren't. Having goals isn't just acquiring the mindset and building the stamina to gain achievement; it's a lifestyle that affects our future and determines our success. Goals do several things for us, like the following:

1. Improves self-image and makes us feel good;
2. Aligns our focus and keeps us focused;
3. Helps us manage achievements in life;
4. Encourages us to act towards our vision;
5. Keeps us responsible and accountable for tracking our progress and;

6. Inspires us to live life to the fullest

From here on, the advantages of sticking to a goal also appear. Since goals are to be incorporated long-term, sticking to them allows a person to continuously strive towards a said goal. Once more, grit is required, tested, and applied. And grit, as discussed in an earlier chapter, is the most accurate identifier for successful people. But what use does grit have if one does not have realistic and feasible plans to achieve goals?

Before goals come objectives. Objectives are daily tasks, weekly activities, monthly lessons, and yearly accomplishments that a person aims to fulfill to achieve a goal. These tasks, activities, lessons, and achievements are part of the plan. Without a plan, your goals are just wishful thinking. It's praying for good health but not eating right, exercising, or sleeping well—purely mental and abstract. So, now, how do we set goals and develop plans? Here's how:

1. *Align your goals with your purpose*

Before purpose, we have our personal values—another factor to consider in setting goals and determining purpose if you have yet to determine it. Our values help us align both our goals and purpose in life. If our plans and visions are not in tune with our core values, the chances are we will quickly lose motivation to achieve them. So, to align your goals and purpose, determine your core values first.

After identifying your core goals, go back to the root of your life's purpose. What empowers you to get out of bed every morning? Then, with your purpose in mind, ask yourself: is my career, personal life, financial capability, family life, social circle, and short-term and long-term plans aligned with my purpose?

To illustrate, let's say you want to own your school. Do you have a degree in education? Are you passionate about teaching? Are you earning enough to build your own school in the future? Is your family supportive of this decision? Are you acquainted with people who can inspire you to achieve this? Are your short-term and long-term plans related to this vision? Finally, are all these tied to your values?

2. *Set SMART Goals*

Setting SMART goals doesn't pertain to intelligent or well-thought-of goals. SMART is an acronym that means Specific, Measurable, Attainable, Relevant, and Time-Bound. This popular goal-setting technique improves your odds of achieving your goals.

Specific, meaning your goals are well-defined—neither broad nor generic, so is the end result you perceive. Measurable in the sense that you can track your progress; has a goal been achieved? How many more milestones are left? Attainable is synonymous with achievable. Will you be able to achieve it? Relevant, as discussed earlier, it must be aligned with your values and your purpose. It must be realistic. Finally, Time-Bound; there is a deadline for your goal. In between the progress and the deadline, you can change, adjust and re-evaluate your plans and the goal itself. What's the feasible timeline? How long will it take to achieve your goal? How much time do you have to spend? These are some considerations.

3. Create an action plan

Every goal requires a plan. The easiest way to craft plans is by defining your objectives and splitting them into manageable tasks or milestones. The key to making an effective action plan is to ensure that each task or activity you write down is related to your goal. Achieving goals becomes much easier if you break them down into short-term and long-term plans with a corresponding and, more importantly, realistic timeline.

Another tip for making this timeline is to prioritize your goals. Which ones can be done today? This week? Next month? Next year? Identify them and prioritize the ones with the closest deadline. Although it's subjective, and can only be identified by you, always consider that you should prioritize the plan, as it actively forms part of achieving your goal. Filter out distractions as goals require focus. Perhaps, you should write a "do's" and "don't" list—one list for the things you must do and one for things you should avoid.

4. Think of those around you

It may sound more sentimental than rational, but thinking of the people around you is also a consideration in goal-setting and planning. Is your goal appropriate or aligned with the values of your partner, children, family, and employees? Considering them will be essential to gaining their support. As always, goals are easier to achieve with a support system.

So, before planning on traveling the world, ask how your partner or children feels about this. If you're expanding your business to a new line of work, ask your co-owners and employees how it will affect them.

5. Take action

All things considered, it's now time to take action based on your plans. There are two things you have to keep in mind when doing this: stick to your plan and build up habits. Since success is determined by your grit, the ability to stick to your plans long-term is a mindset that favors you more. While sticking to it, setting a schedule for accomplishing daily plans has the potential to become a habit. So, make your plans a part of your daily routine until it comes to you naturally.

You can also incorporate the "Eat That Frog" technique, popularized by Mark Twain, quote: "...If it's your duty to eat 2 frogs, it's best to eat the major one first". Simply put, between two tasks, accomplish the biggest, more important one in the morning before proceeding to smaller, less important ones. Additionally, you can also leverage the Pareto Principle if the "Eat That Frog" Technique doesn't work for you. This states that 80% of your outcome come from 20% of your efforts. So, in the application, you must find which actions produce the most significant results.

6. *Manage your time*

Apart from all these, effective time management is at the core of achieving goals. Organizing your time, sticking to your schedule, and checking off daily tasks increase your potential for overall success.

In time management, there are a matrix to take into consideration which are: (1) important and urgent or short-term crises and problems that need to be managed right away, (2) important but not urgent or long-term goals, (3) urgent but not important like avoiding distractions and interruptions, and (4) not important and not urgent or limiting time-wasting activities. Finish activities and tasks based on this matrix.

7. *Track your progress*

You will only know you're on the right track if you check it. Admittedly, distractions are bound to set us off the path, so monitoring your progress, evaluating your performance, and adjusting your plans must be constantly done.

In your checklist of things to do, always cross out activities you finished and short-term goals you have already achieved. Seeing your tasks get crossed off your "vision board" or journal keeps you motivated and excited for D-day.

While putting in the effort on short-term and long-term goals, never forget the bigger picture or the purpose of it all. Always keep yourself connected to your vision and purpose in everything you do, no matter how simple or complicated.

Throughout every step of goal-setting, planning, and taking actions to succeed, remember the "why's." Why am I doing this? Why do I have to achieve this? Why is this success vital to me? And when you lose heart every now and then, recall the first time you decided to set this goal—remind yourself why it mattered to you then and why it should keep mattering to you now.

Section 2: Accelerating Your Journey with Role Models, Mentors And Sponsors

While everyone is talking about how life's journey is so much sweeter with a company, we'll talk about how the journey of success is more progressive with a pivotal company—like role models, mentors, and sponsors. Surely enough, you've heard that engaging with different kinds of people can be beneficial for your personal and career growth. But how do these people really help define your success? Having goals, as emphasized in Chapter 1, can be an improved experience with the right company. Before further discussing this subject, let's explain role models, mentors, coaches, and sponsors.

A role model is a person with particular traits you admire and wish to also have. They may have skills, talents, intelligence, or personality that you respect. A mentor, on the other hand, is one who sits down with you to discuss your personal and career growth, from plans, suggestions, and opportunities. A mentor motivates you to pursue a project and inspires you to keep going. Similarly, a coach is a person who teaches you and helps you improve at something. Besides their knowledge and expertise, mentors and coaches can help you determine your passion and purpose. Finally, a sponsor speaks about you in your absence— not to condemn you but to recognize your efforts and recommend you, for example, for excellence awards and promotions. A sponsor is your vocal advocate, per se.

So, how do these kinds of people help you achieve your goals?

Role models inspire you to become a better version of yourself.

When you admire and respect a particular trait that a person has, you're more likely inclined to imitate and incorporate these traits into your own life. For example, let's say you admire this person because of her excellent social skills, how she walks into the room, how easily she makes friends, and how she can close a deal with a bright smile and a firm handshake. Because you've seen how practical her skills are, you subconsciously try to attain the same kind of demeanor. Unknown to you, you are increasing your chances of succeeding in the workplace.

Mentors and coaches let you know what you need to improve on.

Since mentors want you to do great on something, they push you to strive harder at what you're doing, even if it means they have to pinpoint what you lack. The more important thing is they give you advice on how to move forward from it. It's their goal to guide you in navigating a particular situation in your life or career. So, let's say you want to become a professional actor. To do that, you have to undergo multiple training sessions, where a coach would tell you the most effective technique to use when you have to cry or memorize your lines. After all, they have the knowledge and expertise to impart to you.

Sponsors give you well-deserved opportunities.

A sponsor who believes in you is a sponsor who would advocate for you. Having a sponsor means connecting with someone who values your work ethic or performance and is willing to vouch for you. Since they believe in your qualifications, sponsors can introduce new opportunities for you. And some of these opportunities are stepping stones toward your goal. For example, in your job application, a former college professor can write a recommendation letter to a company you're applying for.

Finding a role model, a mentor, or a sponsor requires the need to identify what and who you need for your development and endeavor. Either way, choosing your preferred "life guide" is a prerequisite. How? First, *find your passion;* determine your likes and dislikes, childhood dreams, and careers you wish to pursue. Once you find it, you can then find a role model, mentor, or sponsor who can assist you in achieving your aspirations.

Second, *find someone who overcame or solved problems similar to yours.* Like every success story, there will always be struggles. Knowing what motivates you isn't enough— having the will to solve problems that come with it is also crucial. By all means, it's best to gather helpful information on who to look up to and reach out to for guidance. A person with experience in your dilemmas can comfort and motivate you simultaneously.

Finally, *learn about other people's journeys.* There is no specific rule on who should be your role model, mentor, or sponsor; the only thing you have to remember is that it must be someone who helps you strive into the person you aspire to be. Once you choose a person to help you in your journey, find out all about their journey, the struggles they overcame, the lessons they learned, and the values they now live with thanks to this said journey.

Be it a role model, a mentor or coach, or a sponsor, these three pivotal characters can impact your life and success significantly. From being an inspiration, a source of motivation, and a semi-philanthropist, our advancement in life can be accelerated by the company we keep. Hence, at the end of the day, building connections and support systems allow us to stabilize our goals.

Section 3: The 80/20 Rule Applied To Your Life, Decision And Actions

Earlier, we briefly discussed the 80/20rule (aka Pareto Principle). In this Chapter, we will be tackling the Pareto Principle not only in goal-setting but also in real-life application, from decision-making to taking action, even to your career, family life, health, relationships, and personal growth.

In its simplest definition, the 80/20 Rule conceptualizes the thought that only *20% of your efforts will make for 80% of your success*. It sounds straightforward, but it requires insight; you have to identify which 20% of your efforts are most productive and will likely lead to success. It accelerates success and makes a person more productive, more effective as a leader, more confident, more efficient with utilizing money and resources, and better at problem-solving and decision-making.

When Italian Economist, Vilfredo Pareto, introduced the principle, he merely noticed that 80% of his harvests came from 20% of his plants. He then realized that 80% of the country's wealth came from 20% of its people. Later on, Dr. Joseph Juran coined the term and expanded the thought by incorporating the "vital few" and the "trivial many." As the saying goes, we must only *focus on the vital few and ignore the trivial many*—this is the equation for success.

We generally think that putting in more effort, investing more money, and giving 110% will lead you closer to success. For example, it's like buying a Ferrari to get to your neighboring city when your old sedan can get you there all the same. It's not about how much we put in that counts; it's about the right amount of action. It's not about the car—it's about driving to get there. In the end, it's all about that 20% effort that helps out with your success.

So, how do you identify which activities are worth 20% of your success? By listing down all your activities and analyzing which ones will contribute more. How? You'll know it's the most important activity if it is the hardest to accomplish but has the highest payoff and reward.

When people are more inclined to accomplish everything all at once, they forget to see what's truly important. Hence, the need to list down your most important activity arises. Some people think that working on the small tasks first can make a huge difference, simply because they're easier to do. This is where another rule will apply: resist the urge to clear up the easier things first. Because easier things have lower payoffs. Remembering the concept of "Eat That Frog," always confront the bigger, most important task first.

If you remain unconvinced, here are some examples of applying the 80/20 in our lives:

Pareto Principle in Relationships

The 80/20 Rule can be applied in different relationships; family, friendships, and even significant others. For example, we may think that the more friends we have, the happier we will be, but this notion is incorrect. In friendships, identify which 20% of your friends will motivate you to become a better person and which 80% distract you from becoming you. Once identified, opt to spend time with this 20%. You'll realize that your life becomes significantly better without insignificant friendships.

In relationships, you have to realize that 80% of your and your partner's problem comes from only 20% of your actions and behaviors. Hence, the small, minor problems between you that could make up 80% of your problems can be irrelevant and need not cause friction within the relationship. Instead, focus on the pressing problems between you and your partner. Simply put, if the real problem is you don't communicate enough, there is no need to mention that you hate his eating habits or that she does not pick up her clothes after a shower.

Pareto Principle in Career

The 80/20 Rule does not promote being busy as being productive; it's the other way around. It promotes a healthy work-life balance as your personal health can affect your career. Hence, time management is important: identify which of your pending tasks, 20% of them, can lead to better income. With more time saved, you can devote it to exercise, relaxation, mental health breaks, and spending time with loved ones.

This also applies to business management. If you're a business owner, you have to understand that 80% of completed work is produced by 20% of your employees. The Pareto Principle can be used to discern which workers increase productivity—knowing these can help improve knowledge and skills among your employees.

Finally, in sales. The key to getting paid more commission is realizing that 20% of your clients determine 80% of your profits. So, it would be better to focus on clients that contribute more to your gain. Since it takes the same effort to work with high-profit and low-profit clients, focusing more on where you can earn is a technique that can improve income generation. Allow yourself to accommodate persons with the same profile to double your income.

Pareto Principle in Success

In accomplishing goals, the 80/20 Rule can be applied to boost your productivity and impact positive results. How? First, write down ten of your tasks and identify which ones can elevate you closer to accomplishment. Ask yourself, "if there's one thing I can do today, which would provide more progress?" After picking the two most relevant tasks, you'll realize that this is the top 20% you need to work on.

Similarly, you can apply this when it comes to problem-solving. First, list your problems and score them each based on their importance. Then, identify the topmost important problems that need to be solved and solve them first. After doing so, the lesser important problems become easier to handle.

Through it all, the 80/20 Rule aspires to bring success in any aspect of our lives through strategic planning and well-distributed efforts. The traditional thought of putting all you've got into a project or career is a recipe for disaster and failure. Not everything you do will make you successful, so it is crucial to determine which ones will.

Section 4: Understanding Cause and Effects & The Compounding Effect in Life

What is cause and effect in life and why it is important to deeply understand this connection?

Imagine if you could predict the future. Imagine how much easier life would be! You'd know for sure what would happen, and when it would happen. You won't have to worry about your investments anymore because you know they will always grow in value or that your stocks will always go up, because you can see the future. And so on... But wait a minute, there is no such thing as predicting the future! The best we can do is try to understand cause and effect in life in order to better prepare ourselves for what may come our way in any given day or time period. Cause and effect are reactions that take place due to specific actions taken. So before taking any action whatsoever, you must always ask yourself does this cause or effect someone else's life in a positive manner? If the answer is yes, then go ahead and do what you need to do. If your answer however, is that it affects somebody negatively, then perhaps that action isn't meant for you right now. The Law of Cause and Effect says that there is a natural law in this world that will reward you for your positive actions and punish you for the negative ones. There are of course consequences to all actions, whether they be positive or negative. In order to come out on top in life, it's important to understand how cause and effect works. It's vital that you don't get discouraged and give up when things go wrong, but rather you should pick yourself up and focus on improving your attitude and behavior, that way you will be sure to live a much happier life.

There are many examples of cause and effect in life, although many times they may not appear connected. Whether it's business or personal relationships

How to plan your life around cause and effect

The importance of understanding cause and effects in life, is it more important than destiny? Can we plan our life around this concept. Cause and effect is a part of every person's life from birth till death. No matter how strong or powerful some people may think they are, the first thing that happens to them when they're born is a cause, and the last thing that happens when they die is an effect. Life is nothing but a series of cause and effects. We have to plan our lives around cause and effect because every choice we make will have an effect on us either short term or long term depending on what it is. From simple things like brushing your teeth to important decisions like marriage, every choice that you make will have an effect on you either short term or long term.

Every day we face little problems in life which may not seem big enough to confront but can be the building blocks of something bigger down the line if they are not handled correctly. These include bad habits such as smoking, drinking, drug abuse or even just skipping out on school work when it's needed for example if your child were to be absent from school without a valid reason for three times this year his grades at the end of term could drop significantly which would affect him later on once he goes into college or university. If you make a choice to drink and drive this would be the cause and the effect would be if you were to get caught your license could be suspended for a number of months, but worst case scenario you could lose your life or someone else's. Bad habits such as these can also affect your health in time, smoking for example it is not uncommon that smokers would develop lung cancer and later on need an organ transplant.

Every decision we make has consequences; we should keep this in mind before we take any actions which might jeopardize our mental and physical well-being. Some other common problems include spending too much money leading to debt, having unprotected sex leading to unplanned pregnancies or STD's or even just choosing friends who will drag you down with them leading to a waste of a promising future, a dropped GPA or suspension from college on the other hand if you choose friends that are positive and help you improve academically it could lead to scholarships or even better GPAs. Your decision has an effect on your life the same way your life will have an effect on your decisions.

We should include our future selves in our daily choices because what we do today can affect how we live tomorrow. However many people focus only on their immediate needs which cause them to make a bad impulsive choice that they would later regret such as smoking, drinking, taking drugs which all of these results in long-term negative effects on a person's health and/or social life. On the other hand, if we included our future selves in our decision-making process by planning ahead and doing what would benefit us long term like studying or working out which could lead to better grades, healthier life, and a bigger paycheck.

If you plan your life around cause and effect it can help you make healthy choices for yourself because you will be thinking about the consequences of every choice that you make. The same way bad decisions made without planning can have long-term effects on your life positive ones planned ahead of time could have positive effects on your life as well either short term or long term depending on how big the decision is. Life is all about cause and effect. No matter who you are, where you're from or what circumstances surround your birth there will always be a cause and effect to your life.

Every choice you make has a consequence. Do not take this for granted, everything from the simplest choice to the biggest decision will have an outcome that will affect you either short or long term. Whether it's choosing friends, what you eat, how much money you'd spend on something or even who you marry if not planned properly these can all lead to long-term negative effects on your life which could be prevented by simply thinking about future consequences before they happen. Make smart choices and plan ahead for a more successful life!

Understanding the compound effect

The compound effect is when a series of small events or choices leads to a bigger outcome. It's important to understand the compound effect because it can have a major impact on our lives. For example, if we make small changes in our habits, we can end up with big results. The compound effect can also be negative, as we see in cases of drug addiction or crime. In these cases, a series of small decisions or choices leads to bigger and bigger problems.

The compound effect is really interesting because it shows you what small decisions can lead to. It's important for us to understand this so that we're not making bad decisions. The compound effect also shows us how powerful our choices are. We often tend to focus on things that are out of our control, but in reality, most of life is up to us! I have found that when I make good decisions and continuously take action, even if there are setbacks along the way, I tend to see better results than the people around me who aren't motivated or don't know much about doing well.

For example, if we focus on something for a while and practice it over and over again, we will get better at it. This is the principle of "deliberate practice." Deliberate practice can be seen in different areas of our lives from sports to career advancement to relationships. In fact, practicing things deliberately has been shown to have a large effect on how well people do in life. One study shows that deliberate practice can make someone twice as likely to become highly skilled in their field! The benefits of deliberate practice are clear: we become better at skills we work hard to improve.

Our choices and decisions have a large impact on our lives. Even small changes to our daily routine can lead to big differences over time! What we focus on is how we spend most of our time. If we make good choices, like practicing something deliberately or setting goals for ourselves, we'll usually succeed big time!

Section 5: Time Management

People who often feel pressured have one thing in common: they think they lack time to get things done. Admittedly, we sometimes wish for more time, especially when there are deadlines to meet. There's so much to do, but only a few hours a day, as some may complain. But the truth is, there are 24 hours, 1,440 minutes, or 86,400 seconds daily. Time is not the variable we can control; it's how we spend it.

Time management is essential and effective as it positively affects people who practice it. Since this part of the book focuses on achieving your goals and furthering towards success, this Chapter becomes even more relevant with practice than just theory. With this, it's best to be reminded that people who manage their time are more productive, motivated, less stressed, and feel better about themselves. As a result, they have more energy to accomplish tasks and more time for themselves. Hence, time management is essential based on your personality, motivation, and self-discipline. Here are five strategies to effectively manage your time:

1. *Spend your time wisely*

Spending time wisely doesn't necessarily mean consuming all your waking hours doing something productive. It simply means you can get your important tasks done within the given or perceived timeframe. A weekly time log can help you monitor your progress. At the beginning of every week, list down the things you have to do then, at the end of the week, evaluate your results. Did you get everything done? Which activities took up most of the time? What time of the day were you most productive? Which aspect of your life requires more time? Identifying these will help you build a better, realistic routine.

In your routine, set priorities because not everything is important and urgent. The secret to gaining control over your time is to reduce the number of tasks at hand by classifying them as urgent, not urgent, important, and not important. In doing this, a to-do list is the easiest way to prioritize. Still, you must ensure these are manageable tasks to avoid overwhelming yourself.

2. *Organize and schedule*

Research reveals that disorganization or clutter negatively impacts a person and results in poor time management. So, get organized. For example, in your bedroom, label things as "to keep," "to give away," and "to toss." Use the labels to identify items to be kept, donated, and discarded. The same goes for your emails; since reading emails take a lot of time, implementing an organizational system to your email will help. Try separating them into folders and flags and color-coding them based on importance and urgency.

Furthermore, a schedule keeps your time organized. Indeed, work and personal life intertwine every now and then. Between business meetings and doctor's appointments, working on a schedule that accommodates professional and personal life is important. For your schedule to be effective, you must know yourself—like when you are most alert and productive. Also, set a block out time for high-priority activities and avoid interruptions during this time.

3. Get help

→ absolute

Time management takes more than just sheer determination and self-discipline. It can be improved by technological assistance and delegation to a trusted individual. By technological assistance, we mean phone applications as modern alternatives to planners, calendars, charts, index cards, or sticky notes. This includes time trackers, time savers, task managers, and habit developers.

If you're no tech wiz, maybe delegating is more for you. Delegating is assigning a task to someone else so you can focus on other, more critical tasks. First, identify which tasks can be set to appropriate persons with the needed skills and experience. Throughout this process, check on that person's progress, provide assistance, and reward them for a well-done job. Freeing up your plate for tasks others can do on your behalf is worth the cost, considering that it saves you time.

4. Avoid time-consuming habits

Putting off tasks for later is something that all of us have done at one point in our busy lives; some tasks are just overwhelming or unpleasant. But, unfortunately, because we procrastinate, tasks we can do now are pushed to a later time—along with other tasks that cramp our schedules. Thus, it must be avoided. Instead, employ Mark Twain's "Eat That Frog" technique or try the "Snowball" technique, whereas, instead of "eating the big frog first," focus on the smaller tasks leading to the larger task. Either way, you have to get things done sooner than later.

Apart from procrastination, one of the worst habits to develop is being swallowed up by a world with many distractions. Hence, avoid activities that waste time, like scrolling through your phone, engaging in small talk, checking emails, or accepting unscheduled phone calls and visits. In time management, sticking to a schedule is essential. Because schedules keep your activities in check.

On this note, don't fall prey to the thought that multi-tasking saves time—it does not. Studies show that you lose more time switching from one task to another. Unlike common belief, multi-tasking compromises the ability to focus and affects productivity. The best thing to do is to focus on the task at hand.

5. *Stay healthy*

Every time management tactic you put in would only be futile if you miss out on these critical variables: staying healthy physically and mentally. Meeting your deadlines means nothing if you leave your state of body and mind in disrepair. Your schedule must include time to relax and rest. Apart from resting, stay off your mobile vices; your digital well-being should also be kept in check. Hence, set a time limit for scrolling through your phone mindlessly. Shut off your devices if you have to.

Remember, poor time management is a significant contributor to stress and fatigue. Sometimes, we are overwhelmed because we fail to prioritize and make schedules to get things done. But, above all, the more important thing is to ask yourself if you have a proper work-life balance.

Section 6: The Best Methods To Prioritize

"How are you?" That's the question you should focus on in this Chapter. Your answer will be relevant in determining how pressured or stressed you are with your current daily routine. So, are you tired? Overwhelmed? Overworked? Do you feel you don't have enough time to complete everything? Are you on the brink of fatigue or breakdown? If so, it may be because you're managing your time ineffectively. If the previous Chapter didn't provide you enough remedy, here is another solution: prioritize.

Prioritizing entails putting one task above another and finishing the most important activity first. To save time and energy, identifying the most important and urgent task beforehand is a valuable skill to develop. Of course, everything can't be equally important or urgent. If it is, none of them are urgent or important. In prioritizing, it's vital to do your activities the right way; this means doing it in a way that increases your productivity and efficiency, lessens your anxiety and stress, and improves your access to opportunities. So, here are some of the best methods to prioritize tasks:

1. *Revisit your purpose*

Prioritizing may seem necessary at this point, but it becomes harder to accomplish when you forget to trace your activities back to your intention. To understand this concept easily, let's say you are trying to lose weight. Before you decide between eating healthy and visiting the gym, you must first go back to why you want to reduce weight in the first place. Is it for superficial reasons or health reasons? From there, you'll be able to write down appropriate tasks or activities like shopping for healthier food alternatives, making a workout routine, choosing your gym, and picking a physical activity to stick to and do religiously. Now that you have your list, it's time to categorize them between "must do," "should do," and "good to do."

Must-do pertains to activities that are highly critical to achieving your goal or objective. This may require more time and resources. Should do is important but not critical since your goal can still be achieved without doing it. Finally, good to do are optional activities that do not really affect the outcome of your goal but are still good to do, as the name implies.

2. Invest your time wisely

Deciding what to prioritize is easier said than done, especially when determining a particular task's importance. A task's importance is based on the gain or benefits you acquire from acting on it. Thus, how much of your investment will return? Recalling that time is unquantifiable in value, it's best to avoid time expenditures. Wasteful time expenditures refer to tasks that are not strictly aligned with your goals—something that requires a lot of time with far too few rewards. For example, suppose you are currently trying to lose weight. In that case, a wasteful time expenditure is walking around a shopping mall, canvassing for workout equipment you cannot afford. Identifying these activities will help you utilize your time effectively and efficiently. The benefit from your invested time can be either short-term or long-term. Regardless, it must contribute to your overall success.

3. Manage your activities

Even when your tasks and activities have all been written down and planned out, it wouldn't matter if you don't act on and manage them accordingly. Some of the most effective management tools are the most practical ones—making a master list, using the Eisenhower Matrix, and Eating That Frog.

The Eisenhower Matrix, as seen below, can be applied when creating a master list and when identifying which "frog" must be "eaten" first:

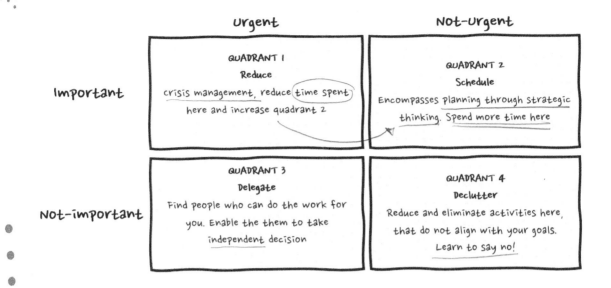

First, making a master list is as easy as it sounds; write your priorities down because keeping them in your head won't always do the trick. A master list will help you identify what has to be done and how soon it should be done. Practically speaking, make a list and tick off items you have already accomplished. Seeing things therein get crossed off also motivates you to keep going. A simple example of this is a simple grocery list. Write a master list with everything that needs to be purchased and find each item, put it in the shopping cart, and cross it out from your list.

Second, the Eisenhower Matrix. In simpler terms, this matrix was made to delegate urgent, not urgent, important, and not important tasks, as depicted in the image above. For example, which items are urgent and important in grocery shopping on a budget? Is it protein or carbohydrates? Meat or ice cream?

Finally, Eat Your Frog Technique. It seems repetitive now, but the best strategy to get things done is to confront the most challenging, most important task first, as already exhaustively discussed earlier.

Through it all, time management is only a part of the many considerations of achievement and success. In reality, life is flawed, and its trajectory can change by the decisions we make. Sometimes, we'll feel pressed for time, miss deadlines, and complete unsuccessful tasks. Still, things get better with knowledge and experience. So, employ these methods for your next project and see how well it works.

Section 7: Deep-Dive on Prioritization Matrices

Prioritization Matrices are good tools to help with prioritizing among a set of options, actions, and so on. They are typically used in a 2x2 format for simplicity but 3x3 can also be used. They offer several advantages, including speed and fast rationalization.

You must choose the terminology that, for your objectives, best fit each axis. Some people make use of the *importance vs. simplicity axes*. Others compare *importance* to *uncertainty*. The Eisenhower Matrix, also known as the *Urgent Important Matrix*, is another matrix type used for prioritization. Prioritization matrices come in numerous variations, but the vertical axis is almost always some variation of More Important vs. Less Important. Finding out the priority is the main objective of these matrices.

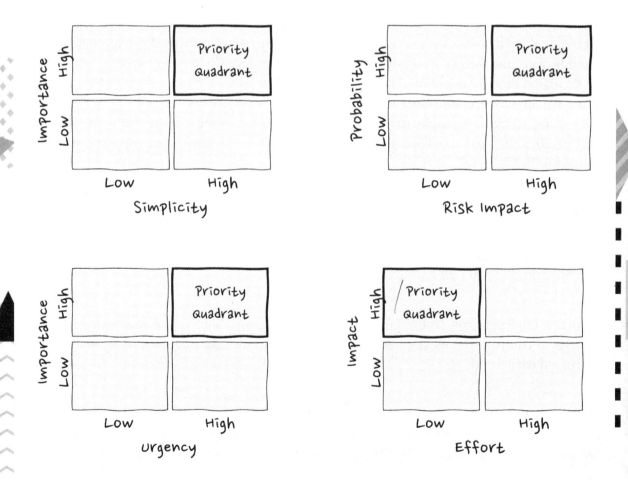

Action Priority Matrix

Actions are placed across effort and impact axes. The way to go about it is to

1) Make a list of the important tasks you want or need to do.
2) Grade these on effort and impact.
3) Arrange the tasks on the Action Priority Matrix per your results.

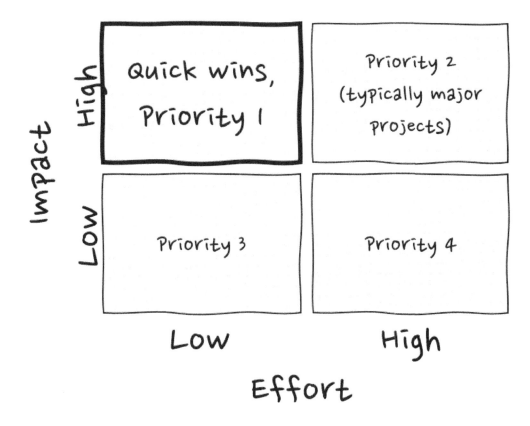

Importance/Urgency aka Eisenhower's Matrix

The Eisenhower Matrix, also known as the Urgent Important Matrix, can help you in selecting and prioritizing activities according to their significance and urgency. It can help you detect less important and urgent jobs that you should either assign to others (delegate) or skip completely.

From 1953 until 1961, Dwight D. Eisenhower served as the 34th President of the United States. He was the Supreme Commander of the Allied Forces during World War II and a general in the US Army before becoming president. Later, he was appointed as NATO's first supreme commander.

Dwight always had to make difficult judgments about which of the several duties he should concentrate on each day. This ultimately inspired him to develop the now-famous Eisenhower principle, which helps us prioritize according to significance and urgency today.

Organizing jobs according to priority and urgency yields four quadrants with various working methods:

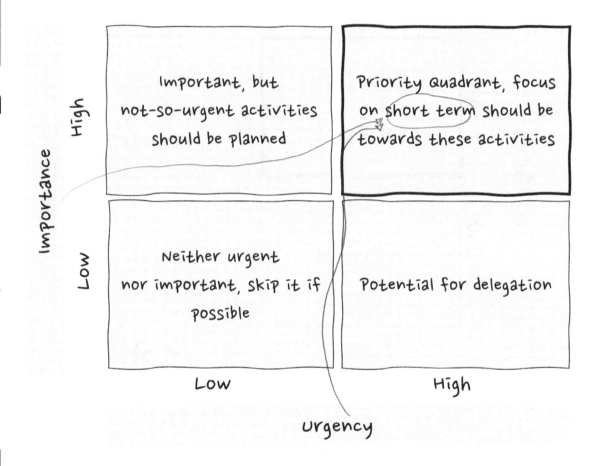

Impact / Probability Matrix

An impact probability matrix is a powerful tool that can be used either for **analyzing risks or opportunities** according to their impact and probability of happening. If we talk about risks, we would refer to it as a *Risk Impact & Probability Matrix*. If we talk about opportunities, we would refer to it as an *Opportunity Impact and Probability Matrix*. But we

must first comprehend what impact and probability represent to fully comprehend how this tool functions.

Finding the likelihood that something will materialize is referred to as risk/opportunity probability. A risk/opportunity will be given a score such as 1, 2, or 3, (Low, Mid, High) in terms of its probability of happening.

Impact assessment refers to determining how the risks or opportunities will affect the state of things or the situation if they were to materialize. We should proceed by assigning scores to grade the impact. For a 3x3 matrix, we would have 1, 2, and 3 (low impact, mid impact, high impact).

The Impact Probability matrix displays the likelihood that a risk or opportunity will materialize as well as its potential effects.

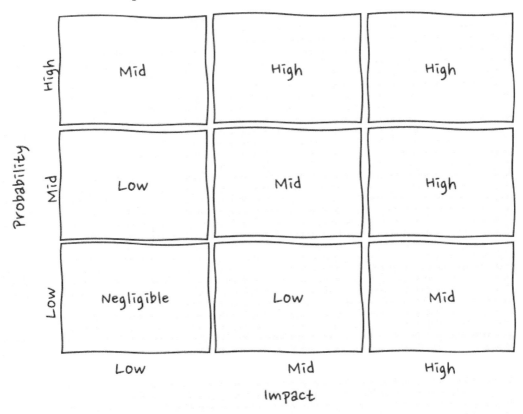

In the top right corner, you will find strong risks or opportunities. In the center are the medium risks or opportunities, and low and negligible risks or opportunities are found in the bottom left corner.

The next conceptual step is to then strategize and define how to address each risk or opportunity given their placement in the matrix. For example, you may choose to:

(R) Resolve, Pursue, or Address the opportunity or risk by minimizing or maximizing the probability and impact, depending on if it is risk or opportunity.

(A) Accept things as they are and take no action.

(T) Transfer the risk or opportunity to a third party. This makes more sense for risk through an insurance mechanism, or in the case of an opportunity that cannot be pursued.

Section 8: The Importance Of Embracing Failure

Everyone will tell you this: you will fail at least once in your life—it happens. But not because it happens to everybody means it feels any less bad. Failures will always be upsetting, no matter what people tell you. Fortunately, our default reactions and emotions are not permanent. With a bit of conviction, you can turn failures into lessons. Before anything else, we must understand that success and failure co-exist.

Failure comes in different forms and "sizes," from losing your job, struggling financially, losing a lover, and failing to complete goals. And disappointment is valid. But what happens if after disappointment comes enlightenment? It becomes growth. This is an essential lesson in embracing failures. Here is some food for thought that is worth remembering whenever your fail:

1. *You still deserve some credit*
   The unnoticed beauty behind failure is the fact that you tried; it means you did a positive action towards a particular goal. Of course, avoiding failure is easier, but inaction embodies a lack of interest or motivation. It's a mindset that successful people don't ever employ. The important thing about failure is you had the courage to do something extraordinary—you deserve credit for that. You may have failed, but you tried. Not everybody tries at all.

2. *You gain experience*
   Overcoming failures is one of the most challenging feats in life. Blame it on peer pressure, societal standards, or the general wiring of the human brain. Still, most of us try again after failing. We fall, get back up, and climb again. When we step out of our safe haven, we gain the confidence to keep doing it. Repeated experience turns to mastery. The next thing you know, failure has brought experience—the experience you need to succeed.

3. You become wiser

The idea of paying it forward does not only relate to kindness or anything synonymous with it. It can also apply to failure. But not literally. What you pay forward or pass on are the lessons you learned from failing. It's nice to have someone looking out for you or heeding warnings. You can be that someone to somebody else. So, don't hesitate to share your story. It may be the much-needed wisdom that someone can use to their advantage.

4. Failure humbles you

Failures only have the power to ruin our progress if we allow them to. One failure is not an indicator of complete failure in that area or anything related to it. Failures are only as devastating as we think they are. If we overgeneralize it, we discourage ourselves from trying again and doing better. In reality, we should allow failure to humble us as it should; they should be reminders that we must always go back to our purpose, no matter how far we've come.

5. Failure allows you to reflect

We are guilty of overthinking where we went wrong; where did I go wrong? How could I have done better? I should have done this—these thoughts tend to pester our minds to the point of restlessness. But knowing that these thoughts are useless and unproductive is not enough. Instead of mere acknowledgment, failure can give you the opportunity to reflect and identify better strategies to succeed next time. For example, we can extract helpful information from failures and try again with better insight.

6. Failure teaches you accountability

If it isn't an unhealthy thinking pattern, we will blame anyone and anything else whenever we fail—it's easier that way. But psychology itself knows that the ability to be accountable for our lapses and mistakes is a positive way of perceiving failures. Therefore, we must realize that we play a role in our failures to correctly identify where we went wrong. Remember, success is never made from blame and regret. It's for improvement.

Failure isn't always a bad thing. Although it's a hurdle we can't jump over, it's always momentary and insignificant; it doesn't have that much power over you. It can only affect us to the level of control we give it. The thing with failure is this: we can always try again. If not, we can find better opportunities. Failure is not the journey's end; it's an opportunity to learn. Even better, one failure comes with six pearls of wisdom, as seen above.

Section 9: Dealing with Procrastination and Strive for better Organization

What is procrastination?

Procrastination is about delaying the execution of tasks that need to be done. The task could be large or small, if you need to do something and put it off, your are procrastinating. The reasons people procrastinate are many and varied: lack of motivation, fear of failure or success, perfectionism. But they all have one thing in common: they give you a false sense of control over your time and work. In reality, delaying can make us feel more out of control than ever before by piling on tasks we don't want to face until later or making us lose momentum when we need that energy for our most important work.

To win this self-defeating game of avoidance, you have to figure out why you go about avoiding doing things in the first place. Why do we allow ourselves to avoid tasks that need attention? There is no simple answer. It could be due to lack of motivation, fear of failure or success, lack of confidence, unclear priorities or time management skills, etc... Whatever the reason(s), there are ways for you to deal with them so that they become less daunting. And once they are done, what follows is a great feeling of accomplishment!

Effects of Procrastination?

Procrastination makes it difficult to meet goals. People tend to go into a state of inaction when they feel unsure about how to proceed, or when things get hard. This is called learned helplessness. It can also happen when people find themselves in an unpleasant situation and just want to get away from the bad feeling as quickly as possible.

What effect does procrastination have on our lives?

Procrastinating can cause problems with performance and productivity at work and home, increasing stress levels and decreasing health and well-being. Using time effectively through task management techniques, prioritizing to-do's, and finding ways to eliminate distractions all play a role in getting the right things done. Procrastinating can lead to inferior results, missed deadlines, damaged relationships and reduced self-esteem.

What can you do to stop procrastinating

There are many ways that you can stop procrastinating. One way is to figure out what is causing you to procrastinate. Once you know what the cause is, you can work on changing your behavior to see if there are any changes in your procrastination. Another way to stop procrastinating is to set a goal for yourself and make a plan of how you will achieve that goal. Finally, you can try using different methods to motivate yourself, such as positive reinforcement or rewards.

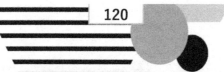

It takes time and effort to find out what is causing your procrastination and work on that issue. If you are serious about breaking the habit, these tips will help get you started.

1) Figure out what triggers your procrastination, like boredom or fear of failure;

2) Set realistic goals for yourself;

3) Make sure this goal isn't too big (or small);

4) Write down why you want to accomplish this goal;

5) Break up tasks into manageable chunks;

6) Reward yourself for completing each task with something fun (not food)

The benefits of overcoming procrastination

There are countless benefits to overcoming procrastination including ease of mind, self-confidence, progress towards long-term goals, and overall better quality of life. Also, it can improve your health by helping you to stay organized and motivated. It can also help you to achieve your career goals by improving your time management skills and increasing your productivity. Additionally, overcoming procrastination can make you a more reliable and responsible employee or a better business person, and can help you to build better relationships with friends and family.

For these reasons and more, overcoming procrastination can be a positive and rewarding experience.

By staying organized, motivated, and on schedule, you are likely to be in better shape than those who let their life slip out of control by postponing tasks. This increased organization can help you to avoid stress and anxiety, which often arise when people try to complete too many things at one time. Additionally, getting ahead on your work gives you more free time during the day--time that might otherwise be spent thinking about tasks that need to get done or attempting to find ways around doing them.

Aside from avoiding stress-related illnesses, people who stay organized are less likely to catch colds or other illnesses because they are generally more aware of their physical health. Furthermore, an organized lifestyle will help you to eat healthier and get more exercise than someone who is typically disorganized with their life.

Staying on schedule can be beneficial for your career because it allows you to complete more work in the same amount of time that others typically do. By getting everything done faster than most people, you will impress your boss or colleagues or succeed in your business.

People who are able to stay on top of their work are likely to have better relationships with co-workers, family members, friends, etc. They will avoid the embarrassment that comes with being late to a work presentation or an event, and can thus improve their reputation among those around them. By staying organized, you also have less time to procrastinate because your days are planned out ahead of time. This could make it easier for you to focus on work rather than getting distracted by things such as social media or television.

The benefits of overcoming procrastination go beyond health and productivity; they also include improved relationships with others. For example, people who complete tasks on schedule are likely to be more reliable and dependable than those who wait until the last minute before working on something important. This shows that you can be counted on and that others can count on you for help in a pinch. In addition, staying organized and on schedule can build your self-confidence because you know that you have the ability to control yourself and accomplish things. And being able to trust yourself is vital in every area of life, including friendships and romantic relationships.

Overcoming procrastination will make you feel as if you have greater control over your life--over what happens to your career, health, love life, etc.--and this feeling can be a major source of happiness.

In summary, overcoming procrastination can lead to many positive consequences in both the short and long term. By remaining organized, motivated, and on schedule, people will be able to protect their health, increase their productivity at work or school, maintain healthy relationships with friends and family members, feel more accomplished as well as happier about themselves and their lives overall. The benefits of overcoming procrastination also include not catching colds as often because you are more aware of your physical health.

Procrastination, Self-Belief and Ambitions

We all understand that there are benefits to working towards an ambition. What many of us fail to see is the connection between mindset and procrastination, which results in us always putting off tasks.

When we set out on a new task, it's important to be aware of our own psychological state. The very act of perceiving ourselves as achieving something gives us pleasure; this is known as the dopamine effect. This, however, often causes problems with procrastinators because they choose instant gratification over long-term rewards.

We often procrastinate because we are afraid. We may fear failure, the negative response of others or even success itself. This can prevent us from starting projects, leaving them to linger on our to-do lists until they become a bigger weight on our shoulders than we can bear.

In order to help overcome these fears, it is important for us to build up a strong sense of self-efficacy. Self-efficacy is defined as an individual's belief that they have the skills and capabilities that enable them to successfully direct their own lives toward their chosen goals.

In other words, if you know what you're doing and think you can actually do something then there's no reason not to start right away! Starting at the very beginning can help you achieve this sense of success.

If the ambition is small enough, then take a moment to reward yourself for taking that first step. It may seem silly or pointless, but this will improve your self-esteem and motivate you to continue being diligent with future tasks. The idea is to build up momentum by rewarding yourself, much like how positive reinforcement works in something like dog training!

Another problem associated with procrastination often arises when we've overfulfilled our own expectations. This can lead us to not want to do any more work because we feel as though it would be too good to be true if all our hard work paid off. Once again, trying to set out a smaller ambition can help overcome this problem because you won't be expecting as much.

Can you see where this leads? We set out small ambitions which are easily achievable, and then we give ourselves rewards when we achieve them. This helps us build up our self-esteem because we feel like we're making progress forward; the result of all this is that our own sense of motivation increases! The more successful you make yourself appear to yourself, the easier it becomes to motivate yourself over time.

It's important to remember that everything takes practice; procrastination is not something that can simply be overcome by reading about it or thinking about its benefits alone. If you are struggling with procrastination, try looking at what may be preventing you from being productive in these certain areas of your life. Once you've done that, it's just about practicing your new skills and building up positive momentum!

Section 10: Why is Now A Good time and How To Gain Momentum In Your Life

In 9th grade, our physics subject taught us that momentum is the measurement of the mass and movement of a particular object—mass multiplied by velocity. But momentum isn't simply a law of motion; it is also a principle of motivation. When taken into present reality, momentum allows you to think rationally and set realistic goals. But as promising as it sounds, we must first learn how to build momentum in our lives.

By now, you've probably overcome emotional and mental hurdles yourself. You once found yourself unable to get out of bed, start an important task, or even finish your meal. Maybe then, everything felt pointless to you. But the fact you're still here means you overcame your troubles—you motivated yourself. And with motivation comes momentum, the ability to become more productive, effective, and efficient. It's building an optimistic outlook alongside the energy required to achieve your goals. In achieving your goals, the main ingredient is the will to get things done now. As the infamous saying goes: "it's now or never." On this note, there are three "It's" you have to remember to build momentum: Do It, Schedule It, and Learn From It.

Do It

The best method to build momentum is to just do it—take a leap of faith and don't hesitate. Whatever it is, starting your project right away is the solution to putting it off and procrastinating. The more you think about it, the more overwhelming it becomes, so just do it. By taking action, you shift your time and energy to the vital task at hand. By theory and practice, the more time and energy you put into something, the more motivated you become. The next thing you know, momentum has been built and feeds itself without much effort from you.

Plan it

If right now is impossible with all the many other things on your plate, give yourself some breathing room to make it work—meaning, set a schedule for when to start doing it. While this feels counterintuitive to the first "It," it's a consideration and not the exception to the rule. Realistically, some things can't just fit into your schedule, but sooner or later, a spot will turn up. So, don't think of it as putting it off—think of it as starting at a better time.

Sometimes, building momentum is not as quick as a freefall; it also requires being submerged or experienced little by little, like dipping a toe in the water before taking a plunge. If it's possible, slowly incorporate tasks and activities into your routine. Do it every single day until it becomes a habit. By the time you notice it, you've made more progress in a week than you did in a month.

Discover It

If you've yet to make amends with your self-motivation and doubts still lingering in the corners of your mind, take your time and build momentum by understanding what you should be doing. Since not all goals are easily achieved, give yourself some slack for taking a few moments to learn and understand your plan. Although it isn't momentum just yet, learning is motivation.

Now that you know the three important "It's" of building momentum, let's illustrate them for better understanding. So, let's say you are writing an essay for school or a report for work. First, try doing it. Just do it. Take your laptop, sit down, and start typing away—whatever comes into your head, put it down and fix it later. It may feel challenging to commit at first. Still, once you've started typing word-per-word, the motivation will flow naturally to you. Your brain responds to your actions, and vice-versa.

However, let's say that you can't do it yet because you have other schoolwork or deadlines to meet. Because of the impossibility of getting it done right now, we'll resort to scheduling it or incorporating it little by little into your schedule. If it's a 3,000-word essay or report, you could maybe spend 30 minutes a day writing 500 words. If not, choose an open time in your schedule, give it a few hours, and work on it then tirelessly.

Finally, if doing it or scheduling it is something you're reluctant about, it's safe to assume that your reluctance comes from the lack of knowledge or skill in getting the work done. If so, allow yourself to learn. Browse related articles on the internet or seek advice from someone with experience writing essays or reports. Within a particular timeframe, absorb what you can. Then when you're ready, get writing.

Although it may seem that building momentum right now is a hard thing to grasp, you are excused from putting too much pressure on yourself, and you are still given a chance to catch up on some things you have yet to learn. Indeed, momentum is an ingredient to success—but it's only one of the ingredients. What matters is your taking a step forward every single time, even if you are unsure of your destination.

Section 11: Eliminate Limiting Belief

All of us go through hardships in life, and when faced with them, we sometimes can't avoid but get discouraged. We start to believe we are inexperienced, incapable, and undeserving—these are examples of self-limiting beliefs. Limiting beliefs are restrictions to one's state of mind. The pessimism and fear it entails could disempower a person from achieving something or experiencing new opportunities, ultimately hindering potential success. Here are some common examples of self-deprecating thoughts:

"I'm not good enough."

"I'm too old or too young for this."

"I don't have enough time to accomplish it."

"I'm not smart enough."

"I'll never be successful."

"I don't have enough experience."

"I'm not talented enough."

"I'll never be the right fit for this job."

These types of unhealthy thinking roots in a place of fear of failure. This chapter aims to help you identify and combat self-limiting beliefs through the following:

1. *Understanding and Identifying Self-Limiting Beliefs*

The initial stage of overcoming limiting beliefs is understanding and identifying the source and its impact on our daily lives. Many people don't know that their negative monologue has been deeply ingrained in their psyche and that it's almost second nature. Hence, awareness is not enough; we must identify where these thoughts are rooted and how much they affect our lives. Ask yourself when and where all these started. If these thoughts are your default response, could you have developed them as a child? What experiences could've triggered it?

Since these "voices" feel like they come from your conscious and subconscious, you may think they are not to be challenged—they should be. While these thoughts plague you from thinking straight and cripple you from acting proactively, you must assess whether or not these beliefs are valid. Most likely, they aren't. Most likely, it's you who brews these thoughts inside your mind. If the problem turns out to be you, the odds of the solution being within you are at a hundred percent. It takes awareness and motivation to alter your inner dialogue.

2. *Developing Better Alternative Beliefs*

Some of the best ways to eliminate limiting beliefs are to replace, challenge, or counter them. By replace, we mean switching to a better dialogue in your head. For example, instead of saying, "I don't have the experience to do this right," say, "I can gain experience from doing this," or "They wouldn't make me do it if they didn't think I could do it."

Another tip is to deliberately challenge these thoughts instead of succumbing to them. If your fear stops you from doing things, try to fight it every now and then. Constantly challenging your fears will make you realize it's nothing to be afraid of. When you catch yourself thinking that you are not enough, incapable, or unworthy, ask yourself: "Am I?"

Finally, countering limiting beliefs. Nothing is more powerful than daily mantras or affirmations; the repetitive reinforcement of positive thoughts helps rewire the mind. Challenge self-deprecating thoughts with mantras like "I am capable," "I am learning," or "I can do this."

3. Resorting to Self-Appreciating Beliefs

Eliminating limiting beliefs is a daily and deliberate practice. After identifying and addressing beliefs that wear out your self-confidence, it's time to actively avoid thinking negatively. Since this cycle is mental, breaking it is up to you. These are three things you have to remember when your old beliefs creep behind you: one, you are worth it. Whatever it is that's triggering limiting beliefs, don't beat yourself up. Instead, appreciate yourself for coming this far—for every little thing you've done to get here. Do it as many times in a day until it becomes a habit. Two, you are the editor of your manuscript called life. When life happens, and it doesn't take kindly to you, remember that you can regain control. Whatever happens, you control the trajectory of your life. Three, you're meant to move forward. Whatever past experience or emotional baggage you carry with you, don't let it stop you from your progress. If you want to change your narrative, change it. If you wish to improve your life, live your best life. After all, you've come this far, and you deserve it.

Limiting beliefs are purely personal judgments that are often backed by false premises. Blame chemical imbalances in the brain, the environment you grew up in, or the values instilled in you as a child. Still, at the end of the day, the choice to work through this mindset is something only you can decide on. So, work on your self-awareness and self-esteem. Be your own cheerleader because if you don't believe in yourself, why should anyone believe in you?

Section 12: How To Solve Any Problem

Is life really life without problems? If anything, the only constant thing in a world that continuously changes is problems—but this isn't always a bad thing. Although it has a negative connotation, problems are vital to growth and learning. Looking back now to the things you overcame, you'd realize you wouldn't be here if it weren't for your old problems. You're wiser and better, thanks to bitter experiences. As early as now, we shouldn't allow ourselves to succumb to self-limiting beliefs just because we have problems. But don't be confused between coping and solving problems. While most people choose to just cope with problems, what needs to be done is to solve problems. Coping alone does not change anything about bad situations; in reality, you only sweep it under the rug or hide it in the closet along with your other unattended "skeletons." Admittedly, coping is a relevant life skill, but resorting to it alone won't improve your situation. Hence, the necessity of problem-solving.

So, in a world bombarded with distractions that stop you from facing problems head-on and are filled with multiple choices that hinder you from making the confident answer, how do you effectively solve problems? By following this step-by-step guide:

1. Acknowledge and identify the problem

Let's admit it's easier for us to ignore problems and never circle back around to solving them. But such a non-confrontational trait is not an impressive problem-solving tactic—it's the worst. So the first step to solving problems is acknowledging that there is a problem. Hence, state the problem. Look at it dead in the eye and let it know you know about it. Allow yourself to identify what the problem is.

For example, if the problem is your inability to save money, acknowledge it. Then, identify where the problem is coming from. Is it because your lifestyle is lavish? Is it because you're high on credit? State all of them and be specific about them. What kind of behavior, circumstances, and timing affects your problem? Are you an impulsive shopper? Do your friends influence you easily to spend? Were there any events this month that required you to spend that much? Acknowledge and identify each one of them.

2. List down possible solutions

Great, now you managed to identify what the problem is. Now, it's time to confront it—not thoughtlessly, though. Confront your problems by preparing for them. So, list down all possible solutions.

Frequently, the need to come up with solutions stops us from coming up with just the best solution. In reality, the quality of your solution is irrelevant. In this stage, all you have to do is list down more than ten solutions. Get creative, be resourceful, and don't overthink it. Simply come up with solutions to your problem, including solutions you won't naturally come up with.

Who knows? Maybe what's unconventional for you is the most effective one for the situation. This process aims to avoid limiting yourself from your usual thinking patterns.

Using a similar illustration as the above example, the possible solutions to saving money can be making a weekly or monthly budget, setting aside an amount for savings and emergencies, making a time deposit, or finding a person who will keep you accountable.

3. Evaluate listed solutions

Although we encourage creativity in coming up with solutions, we discourage pointless and ridiculous ones. Hence, it's time to rack your brain and consider whether the solution you listed is helpful. In each one of them, consider the pros and cons. Then, eliminate the ones that won't help at all. It may seem counterintuitive, if not additional work, but finding the right solution to your problems isn't supposed to be easy.

After eliminating solutions and writing down the pros and cons, write down the remaining solutions in the order of your preference. This way, you can confront your problems with more than one possible solution. Yes, you've identified one solution you want to stick to—your number one solution as you preferred—but having alternative solutions can also help. So, if your preferred solution is to set aside money, it would be best to also prepare a budget or make a deposit account just in case you lack the self-discipline to stick to this solution.

4. Decide on and implement your solutions

The secret to solving your problems is sticking to your preferred solutions. Granted that you now have options, specifying who takes action, how it will be implemented, and when it will be implemented will lead you a step closer to your desired outcome. You can go through your solutions from least preferred to most preferred or vice-versa—the only important thing is you implement them no matter what.

Hence, set aside the money for your savings on your next payday. If it doesn't work, make a budget and try to stick to it. If it still isn't as promising as expected, open a time deposit or a passbook account, and so on. Try all your listed solutions and see which works best for you. Unlike the idealistic belief that each problem has one solution, some problems, half of the time, are meant to be solved by trial and error.

5. Assess the outcome

While trying out every solution, if applicable, assess if the said solution is effective and beneficial. Is your current action plan working, or does it need to be refined? Can it be refined, or does it need to be changed completely? As much as we'd like problem-solving to be a one-way street, reality dictates that it's an intersection with many different routes and many more outcomes. On that note, don't be afraid to fail and start again. The paradox of choice can only paralyze you if you see it as an overwhelming affair and not an opportunity to reset.

Since problem-solving is a part of daily life, developing this skill can help you alleviate overwhelming feelings when confronted with issues. This specific and systematic process of solving problems has the potential for successful solutions. Realizing that some problems require tedious processes such as this lets you prepare your mind for the impending stress and even minimize it.

Section 13: How To Unlock Your Inner Energy

So, you slept eight hours last night, maybe more. You went out for a jog and had a balanced breakfast. You showered and made your bed. You showed up to work on time and met your deadlines. You did everything right—but why do you still feel empty? Miserable? Unmotivated? Detached? If you're wondering what's wrong with you, it may be because your inner energy is low on "fuel." Like a car that stops from running when low on gas, your body slows down and maybe even stops completely when it's low on inner energy or your so-called life force. Apart from blood, it's that thing that flows throughout your body; it fuels your thoughts, actions, and emotions. In different countries, it's called chi, prana, or spirit—it's either psychological or spiritual. And it can be both. It's up to you.

Michael Singer, author of "The Untethered Soul," explains that inner energy does not feed on food or reenergize on sleep. Instead, it responds to you, allowing it to flow freely inside you—through meditation, awareness, and deliberate efforts. Therefore, the culprit to your low inner energy is not the external factors around you but within you. Blocking this can manifest as physical pain, emotional distress, and mental instability. The thought of becoming vulnerable is a scary thing; hence, here are some tips to unlock, restore, and recharge your inner energy:

1. *Manage stress*

One of the main culprits of low inner energy is stress-induced emotions. Unlike physical exhaustion, stress takes a more significant impact on a person's energy. Apart from disturbing the natural flow of your life force, stress can completely deplete it to the point of false helplessness—giving up and no longer trying to get better. Thankfully, there are different methods to control stress; talking to a friend, joining a support group, seeing a psychiatrist, and even engaging in therapy.

Some relaxation therapies include meditation, mindfulness, self-hypnosis, tai chi, yoga, aromatherapy, and acupuncture. Other methods also include straightforward efforts like exercise and journaling and creative ones like aura clearing and crystal meditation.

2. Create a work-life balance

Fatigue steals your life force—this is a known fact. And one of the primary reasons for fatigue is overworking. When it comes to obligations, some people can't simply draw the line between work and life. From being an outstanding professional in your field or a person who can't say no to social obligations, overworking yourself can drain your inner energy. Thus, it is essential to maintain a work-life balance. In addition, it is vital to streamline your activities between professional and personal, priority and not priority.

Allow yourself some room to transition from that model employee to a loving spouse and parent and to just you. Then, your work, family, and self should be able to co-exist without interrupting each other to the point that it exhausts you.

3. Adopt a healthy lifestyle

You've heard this before, but having a healthy lifestyle affects your mood, emotions, perspective, and, ultimately, your inner energy. Engaging in actions that threaten your health, like smoking, sleeping too much or too little, eating a lot of sugar, binge-drinking alcohol, or being dehydrated, all affect your overall wellness.

While it's true that your inner energy is a state of mind, your mind can't work well if it's stimulated by nicotine, sleep-deprived, high on glycerin, sedated by alcohol, or lacks the nutrients that water provides. The thing is, the mind and the body go hand-in-hand in terms of lifestyle.

Although inner energy is sometimes considered pseudo-science, there are moments in our lives when biology cannot explain our exhaustion. Understanding that our inner energy is affected by external and internal factors is key to unlocking our well-needed life force. In terms of the body and the mind, one is the same. Allow them to work synchronously to open up the free flow of inner energy that contributes to your happiness and motivation.

In whatever professional or personal endeavor you are partaking in, remember that the twin kinship of the body and the mind similarly requires wellness. While this Chapter focuses on inner energy, it also applies to the previous chapters in that endurance requires energy—to overcome struggles, one must have the physical and mental fitness for it. Finally, energy is needed to set and achieve goals, gain inspiration, embrace failure, solve problems and motivate oneself.

Conclusion

Mental fitness and emotional regulation are delicate things vital to an individual's physical, psychological, social, and even financial development or overall personal growth. The journey to understanding the self is not linear, as this book has presented. From understanding the mind, rewiring the brain, finding your purpose, and setting up goals, this book aspires to provide insight that could be translated into different layers of confidence and contentment; some of the few factors that affect happiness and overall wellness. Thus, here is a brief summary of the concepts we have tackled so far:

Understanding & Solving Overthinking

To reiterate, the mind is both exquisite and complicated. Apart from being the body's powerhouse that receives information and reacts to stimuli, it is also in charge of other mental activities like thinking—that sometimes becomes too much to the point of inducing anxiety. Since overthinking is tedious and futile, we must actively find ways to prevent or lessen it through guided visualization, grounding techniques, and asking our subconscious mind, as discussed previously. Guided visualization is a ten-minute mental exercise to ease fatigue. Grounding techniques is to promote mindfulness through the use of the five senses. And asking the subconscious mind to communicate with yourself deeply and gather unsolicited answers without interpreting them.

On the other hand, mental clutter is the presence of multiple negative thoughts in your mind, disallowing you to acquire mental peace and clarity. Caused by information overload, the paradox of choice, and pessimism, it tends to overwhelm you and, in turn, encourages procrastination. Some ways discussed in decluttering the mind include decluttering your physical environment, sleeping, relaxing, meditating, starting a journal, setting priorities, limiting information intake, and being firm with decision-making.

Mastering and Controlling Your Emotions

Emotions are significant in understanding the self. As a subconscious state of mind, emotions identify how we feel about a particular situation: joy, sadness, surprise, contempt, disgust, and anger. Since emotions likewise trigger feelings, actions, and decisions, it is crucial to balance emotion and logic. To be logical, you must understand what really matters in life, take advantage of the wheel of life, and identify your purpose. Relatively, Ikigai pertains to the joy of living a meaningful and purposeful life. Accordingly, its 10 guidelines are as follows: keep moving, take it easy, avoid overeating, be among friends, get in shape, smile, get back in touch with nature, offer gratitude, be present in the moment, and do what makes you happy.

To achieve the peak state of our emotions, we must divulge the elements surrounding them, which are physiology, focus, and language.

Under physiology, your body affects the mind, and vice-versa. For example, your food can affect your mood, or your posture can boost your confidence. For focus, your attention should be around the things you can control, things you have, things you can do, the balance between your past, present, and future, things you need, things that are good, and things that are your goals. Lastly, for language, how you speak to yourself affects you—so do it with kindness. Even empowering questions could affect your state of mind, whereas instead of asking, "why do I perform poorly?" Instead, ask, "What is the smartest way I can solve my problems?"

In the end, your emotional state depends on how you use it—and it must be to your advantage, even if it requires you to take responsibility, choose the right emotions, practice awareness, and give better meanings to the situations surrounding you. Sprinkling optimism in your life can change its trajectory for the better.

Setting up the Bases for Growth

Instead of skills, physical traits, and IQ, the main predictor for success has been identified as grit—the determination to pursue long-term goals. With this in mind, we differentiated a fixed mindset from a growth mindset. In a fixed mindset, people perceive that their skills and intelligence are innate, while those with a growth mindset think that skills and intelligence can be enhanced with effort. For the former, it's saying, "I simply have no talent for singing." And the latter being, "If I take vocal lessons seriously, I can sing well." A growth mindset can be developed by starting small, understanding success and failure, taking it easy on yourself, and changing your outlook on life. Relatively, a growth mindset is conditioned for optimal success. And success can be developed gradually through different approaches, including empowering routines, improving your self-image and self-confidence, and thinking big.

Likewise, with success comes failures. Thus, it is equally important to understand that problems are opportunities in the guise of challenges. The one thing successful people share is the ability to handle problems with a positive perspective, as problems are outlets for learning, improving, and growing. Be it success or failure, incorporate an attitude of gratitude, as it also shifts your mindset and enhances your well-being.

Make It Happen

For success to come to life, goals must be set—not just set, but stuck to and worked on. As a matter of fact, goals do more than just encourage us, they also improve our self-image, align our focus, help us manage achievements, keep us accountable, and inspire us to live our lives to the fullest. How? By aligning your goals with your purpose, setting SMART (Specific,

Measurable, Attainable, Relevant, and Time-Bound) goals, creating an action plan, thinking of those around you, taking action, managing your time, and tracking your progress.

But the journey to success will always be sweeter with company—relevant companies, like models, mentors, and sponsors. They're someone who can inspire you, give advice on what you can improve on, and vouch for you because they believe in you.

Some of the most effective ways to achieve goals include the Pareto Principle, or the 80/20, time management, prioritizing, identifying which tasks are urgent, not urgent, important, and not important, also known as the Eisenhower Matrix, or employing the Eat Your Frog Technique.

At this point, it may seem redundant. Still, embracing failures allow you to realize some essential life lessons, such as having the courage to try again, gaining experience, becoming wiser, staying humble, allowing self-reflection, and developing accountability. On the other end, problems are not to be avoided nor simply coped with; they must be solved. Even with the odds of failing and encountering problems, build the momentum to do things now— because now is the perfect time to get things done. Additionally, believing in yourself ultimately eliminates limiting beliefs—beliefs that make you think you are inexperienced, incapable, and undeserving.

At the core of your emptiness or demotivation, perhaps what needs to be solved is something within you—your inner energy or life force. You can unlock, restore, and recharge this by managing stress, creating work-life balance, and adopting a healthy lifestyle.

Final Words

As the mind controls most of our lives, ensuring our mental health is in top-notch shape is a significant factor in our quality of life. We may think mental fatigue and anxieties are "all in the mind," but in reality, they can determine if we live our life to the fullest—by confronting problems, planning ahead, setting goals, and succeeding.

It is exhausting to think that life has a lot of requirements to attain contentment and happiness, but it's the better alternative than living an unfulfilled life, empty and detached. So, work on yourself. Take care of yourself, physically and mentally.

How Can You Get the Best Out of This Book

To get the maximum benefits out of this guide we recommend the followings:

1) Use mind maps to absorb well the key concepts
2) Use memory techniques such as Memory Palace to retain the key info
3) Practice, Practice, Practice
4) Adopt the Feynman technique and try to educate with what you have learned someone unaware of the topic.

How to Get Your Free Gift

To further complement your knowledge please download the ebooklet

☑ *Understand Your Personality - Intro to Personality Type Theories*

→ **To get it scan the following QR Code**

Or go to

https://bigrocksgroup.com/brilliant/